CISTERCIAN STUDIES SERIES: NUMBER ONE HUNDRED TWENTY-EIGHT

WHOLLY ANIMALS
A BOOK OF BEASTLY TALES

David N. Bell

CISTERCIAN STUDIES SERIES: NUMBER ONE HUNDRED TWENTY-EIGHT

WHOLLY ANIMALS
A BOOK OF BEASTLY TALES

by
David N. Bell

Illustrated by
Alice Duthie-Clark

Cistercian Publications
Kalamazoo
1992

The work of Cistercian Publications is made possible in part
by support from Western Michigan University to
The Institute of Cistercian Studies.

Library of Congress Cataloguing-in-Publication Data:

Wholly animals : a book of beastly tales / [compiled and translated
by] David N. Bell.
    p. cm. — (Cistercian studies series ; no. 128)
    Includes index.
    ISBN 0-87907-328-4 (alk. paper). — ISBN 0-87907-628-3 (pbk. :
alk. paper)
    1. Animals—Religious aspects—Legends.   2. Saints—Legends.
I. Bell, David N., 1943–   . II. Series.
BL439.W546   1992
291.2'12—dc20   92-8486
                                             CIP

Typeset by Photo Composition Service.   *Printed in the United States of America.*

This book is for
Pasha and Jenny-Fur in St John's;
Paddington in Rochester;
Tippi, Tom-Pet, and Rosie in Kalamazoo;
Mimi and Whitney in Seignelay;
and Gribouille of Pontigny.

'Love of cats is part of faith'
Muhammad

TABLE OF CONTENTS

PREFACE

Most of us are grateful to Noah for his foresight in building the ark. Had he not done so, this world would certainly be a cleaner and quieter place, but also one of less interest and excitement. His own task was no small burden, for we know from a Midrash that he was occupied twenty-four hours a day for a whole year in attending to the various animals which were committed to his care. Each had to be fed at the proper time and each needed its own particular food: straw for the camels, barley for the donkeys, vine tendrils for the elephants, glass (*sic*) for the ostriches, and so on. The results, however, were fortunate, for if we overlook for the moment the indignities and depredations inflicted on it by the human race, this world of ours is a world blessed with an astonishing variety of creatures from ants and aardvarks to zebus and zebras.

The stories told in the following pages deal with only a few examples from this multitudinous creation, and most of the human beings who also make their appearance represent the best of their kind. They are not, of course, typical of the race, and no animal who reads this book should assume that there are any others like them. The vast majority of people have mistreated, mutilated, abused, starved, tortured, maimed, disfigured, sold, killed, and eaten the representatives of the animal creation for the last several thousand years. They are still doing so now, and there is no reason to assume that they will cease to do so in the immediate—or indeed distant—future. The lives of men and women on this planet may not be so short as once they were, but they are still, for the most part, nasty and brutish; and it is with some relief that I turn from the contemplation of fallen humanity to a selection of tales of unfallen animals.

The stories translated here are to be found in sources in Arabic, Aramaic, Catalan, Coptic, German, Greek, Hebrew, Italian, Latin, Persian, and Yiddish. It would have been possible to go further east and include many tales from Buddhism and Hinduism, but one has to stop somewhere. The Jātaka tales alone—the stories of the Buddha in his previous incarnations—would provide enough material for a whole volume of this size. But even as it is, I felt I could not properly restrict myself simply to the Christian tradition (for the history of the relationship of animals and Christianity is singularly bleak), but have introduced here and there, as leaven to leaven the whole lump, an occasional tale from Judaism and Islam as well. The Judaeo-Christian-Muslim tradition is, after all, concerned with one and the same God (though most seem unwilling to admit it) and one and the same creation, and it seemed only appropriate that the most important representatives of all three streams—Moses, Jesus of Nazareth, and Muḥammad—should find a place in these pages.

In the great majority of cases, however, I have restricted myself to Christians (for that is what I was asked to do), and of these Christians most were 'saints'. The nature of sanctity is not something I intend to discuss in these pages (save to point out that it is gravely misunderstood); but to make it clear that we are not restricting ourselves entirely to the formally canonized, I have included one or two nonsaints as well. Here, too, good tales could be told of non-Christians as well as Christians: a splendid example being the story of the founding of the capital of Egypt by 'Amr ibn al-'Āṣ.

When 'Amr invaded Egypt in late 639, the country was rapidly subdued by the Muslim armies; but by 641 only half the conquest had been accomplished and 'Amr was eager to complete it. He therefore ordered his army to begin the advance northwards to Alexandria. But when they were about to take down his tent, they found that a dove had made her nest on top of it and there laid her eggs. 'Let her be,' said 'Amr (and I am here following the account in Yāqūt ibn 'Abd Allāh al-Ḥamawī), 'for she has taken refuge under our protection. The tent shall remain here until her chicks are hatched and she herself has flown away.' And he ordered a guard to be left at the tent to ensure that the dove would be unmolested. In due course a settlement was established on the same site and became known as Fusṭāṭ, which, according to one tradition, can be interpreted as 'the town of the tent'. For many years it functioned as the administrative capital of Egypt and was, in essence, the seed from which developed the modern city of Cairo. But if we began to tell tales of this nature, our work, and likewise our book, would be endless.

A number of the stories which appear here also appear in Helen Waddell's delightful compilation, *Beasts and Saints* (London, 1934). The overlap is, however, only partial: many of the tales which appear here do not appear there, and some which appear there do not appear here. But all of them have been re-translated and it is I who am solely responsible for any errors. It might, therefore, be wise to say a word or two about the translation technique. All the stories in the first part of the book are translations, not paraphrases. Some paraphrases do occur at the beginnings of the various tales in order to put them in perspective, but these are enclosed in square brackets so that one can see what's what. Nevertheless, since this is not an academic treatise, I have translated the several extracts a little more freely than I would have done in other circumstances, and have not hesitated to add an explanatory word or phrase here or there in order to make the sense of the story clearer. The animals themselves sometimes appear as he, sometimes as she, and sometimes as it, depending on the context. I do not myself ever think of an animal as an 'it' (except after spaying or neutering [an operation from which the majority of human beings would undoubtedly benefit]), but English, like Coptic, sometimes has problems with its prepositions and if we simply say 'he bit him', we sometimes cannot tell whether the dog is biting the saint, or the saint the dog. In the second part of the volume, where one can read something of the lives and characters of the holy men and women with whom we are concerned, a number of further stories appear, but they are mostly retold and are not intended to be straightforward translations.

Finally, this book is not intended primarily to be a book with a message. But as Helen Waddell said more than fifty years ago: 'If the dark places of the earth have always been full of the habitations of cruelty, there has always been a spring of mercy in mankind' (*Beasts and Saints*, xix); and if that spring still runs, and if any one of the tales here translated serves to make it run a little faster, I shall have been more than rewarded. But twenty years involvement with the Society for the Prevention of Cruelty to Animals does not imbue one with much confidence in the capacity of the human race to change for the better.

DNB

PART I

THE ANIMALS

AN INTRODUCTORY TALE

[At the great court of the animals (which seems a proper place to begin this book), the ox said to the lion, the king of beasts, that a certain snake had told him that of all the animals, the most wicked and the most false in the whole world is surely the human race. The lion then asked the ox to tell him the snake's reason for saying this, and the ox told the following tale:]

It happened once that a bear, a crow, a man, and a snake fell down a well. A holy man, a hermit, passed by the place where the well was, and when he looked in, he saw all four of them there in the well, and they could not get out of the well. All of them together begged this holy man to pull them out of the well and each one promised him a good reward. So the man pulled up the bear and the crow and the snake from the well, but when he wanted to pull out the man, the snake said that he should not do so, because if he did, he would receive an ill recompense. The hermit, however, was unwilling to believe the advice given him by the snake and pulled the man out of the well.

The bear then brought the holy man a hive of bees, full of honey, and when the hermit had eaten all that he wanted of the honey, he set off for a certain city where he intended to preach. When he entered the city, the crow brought him a precious tiara: a tiara which belonged to the king's daughter and which the crow had taken from her head. The hermit took the tiara with great delight, for it was very valuable.

Soon afterwards a man went through the city proclaiming that if the person who had that tiara would return it to the king's daughter, she would give him a great reward; but if anyone had hidden the tiara and would not tell where, he would receive a very great punishment.

The good hermit then came to a street where he found the man whom he had brought up from the well, and the man happened to be a silversmith. The holy man gave the tiara secretly to the silversmith, but the silversmith took it to the court and accused the holy man. The holy man was then taken, beaten, and imprisoned.

Then the snake which the holy man had brought up from the well came to the king's daughter while she was asleep and bit her hand. The king's daughter cried out and wept, for her hand was all swollen. The king was incensed at the sickness of his daughter, her hand being so inflamed and poisoned, and he had it proclaimed throughout the whole city that anyone who could cure his daughter would receive great gifts. The snake then went to the king while he was asleep and whispered in his ear that there was a man locked up in the court prison who possessed a herb which would cure the king's daughter. This was a herb which the snake had earlier given to the holy man; and he had also given him instructions to put it on the hand of the king's daughter and, at the same time, to ask the king to render justice on the silversmith who had paid him back with such an ill recompense. This he did, just as the snake had commanded, and the holy man was released from prison and the king did justice upon the silversmith.

[The lion and his court were delighted with this story, and the lion then asked the ox if he thought it wise to fear a human ruler. The ox said to him: 'It is extremely dangerous to be at enmity with a human ruler, for no animal can defend itself against a person who is wicked, powerful, and crafty.' Animals all, take note!]

AN ANONYMOUS MONK OF
THE LAVRA OF ABBA PETER

Who Fears Whom?

Abba Polychronius the Priest told us that another old man, who was living in the lavra of abba Peter, would often go out and stay on the banks of holy Jordan; and when he found a lion's den, there he would sleep. One day he found two lion cubs in a cave, carried them into the church in the cloak he was wearing, and said: 'If we keep the commandments of our Lord Jesus Christ, these animals will be afraid of us; but through our sins we have become slaves, and it is we, rather, who are afraid of them'. And the brothers returned to their caves with great profit.

AN ANONYMOUS MONK OF FONDI

The Thief and the Snake

In the monastery of Fondi there was a monk of the most exemplary life who was also the gardener. But there was a thief who used to come and climb over the fence and secretly carry off the vegetables. So when the gardener found only a few of these where he had planted many, and noticed that

some had been trampled underfoot and others plundered, he
went round the whole garden and found the way the thief
used to get in. Then, walking
further in the garden, he also
came across a snake. 'Follow me',
he commanded. And when he
came to the thief's way in, he
gave the snake its orders, saying:
'In the name of Jesus, I command
you to guard this entrance and
not to allow the thief to come through here'. The snake immediately stretched itself out full length across the path and the
monk returned to his cell.

At noon, when all the brothers were resting, the thief
came as usual and climbed the fence. But when he had one
foot in the garden, he suddenly saw that his way was blocked
by the length of a snake. In his terror he fell backwards, but
his shoe got caught on a stake in the fence and he had to hang
there upside down until such time as the gardener should
return.

When the gardener arrived at his usual time and found
the thief hanging on the fence, he said to the snake: 'Thanks
be to God, you have done what I told you. Now you may go'.
And it immediately crawled away. He then went to the thief
and said: 'What's this, brother? God has handed you over to
me. How did you dare to come so many times and steal the
fruits of the monks' labours?' And saying this, he freed his foot
from where it was caught in the fence and lowered him to the
ground without injury. He then said: 'Follow me'. And with
him following, he led him to the entrance of the garden and
with great sweetness there presented him with the vegetables
he had been trying to steal. 'Go,' he said, 'and do not steal
again. But if you are in need, come here to me and I will give
you with devotion what you are trying to take with sin'.

TWO ANONYMOUS MONKS IN EGYPT

The Desert In Bloom

When I first went into the desert about twelve miles from the Nile (I had one of the brothers as a guide, someone familiar with all the places) we came to a certain old monk living at the foot of a mountain. There was a well there, something extremely rare in those parts. He had a single ox whose only labour was to turn the wheel on a machine which would bring up water, for the well was said to be a thousand or more feet deep. There was a garden there, too, well supplied with all sorts of vegetables, and this is something contrary to nature in the desert, where everything is so parched and dried up by the heat of the sun that it never bears seed or puts forth the tiniest root. But in this case, the holy man shared the labour with his animal and their industry bore its proper fruit: the regular irrigation of water gave such richness to the sand that we saw the vegetables in this garden growing and flourishing in a wholly wonderful way. On these they lived, the ox and his master, and from this abundance the holy man provided a meal for us as well.

After the meal, as evening was drawing nigh, he invited us to a palm-tree about two miles away whose fruit he sometimes used. But when we came to the tree to which our kind host was leading us, we came upon a lion. When we saw him, I and my guide trembled with fear, but the holy man walked on without any hesitation. We, therefore, followed him—but very nervously! The wild animal discreetly withdrew a little way (one could see here the command of God) and stood there while the old man picked the fruit which was hanging on the lower branches. He then held out a handful of dates, and the beast ran up and took them as freely as any animal round the house; then, after he had eaten, he went away. We watched this, still trembling, and we could easily see how great was the power of faith in him and how weak it was in us.

Penitence

We saw another man, equally remarkable, who lived in a little hut which could hold only one person at a time. It was said of him that a she-wolf used to come and stand near him while he was eating: the beast never failed to come to him at the proper time for the meal, and she would wait outside until he offered her whatever bread was left over from his frugal repast. She would then lick his hand and go away, as if she had given him comfort and thereby fulfilled her mission.

But it happened once that the holy man had gone off with a brother who had come to visit him and he was away for a long time, not get-ting back until it was night. The beast, meanwhile, had come at the usual time for her meal, and when she sensed that her friendly patron was not there, she went into the empty cell and looked around inquisitively to see where its inhabitant might be. Hanging there, just within reach, was a little basket of palm-leaves containing five loaves, and she presumed to take one and eat it; and then, having perpetrated this wicked deed, she made off.

When the hermit returned, he saw that the little basket was broken and noticed that the number of loaves was not the same. He perceived the loss of his household things, and near the door he recognised little pieces of the stolen bread; nor was there much doubt in his mind as to the identity of the thief. But as the days went by and, contrary to her custom, the animal did not appear (for she was too conscious of the audacity of her deed to come under false pretences to the one she had wronged), the hermit was deeply grieved that he had lost the comfort of his adopted child. But after he had prayed for her return and after the seventh day had gone by, she again appeared when he was eating, just as she had done in the past. But in her embarrassment and penitence (both of which were obvious) she did not dare approach him: her eyes were fixed on the ground in profound shame and it was quite evident that she was entreating his forgiveness. The hermit had pity on her confusion and commanded her to draw near: he stroked her sad head with a caressing hand and then refreshed his penitent with twice the number of loaves she had stolen. And once she had received forgiveness, she put aside her grief and resumed her customary office.

BARTHOLOMEW OF FARNE

Prey and Predator

There was a little bird which used to come each day and take grain from his table, and then, when it had finished its meal, it would fly away. One day, when Bartholomew was busy fishing, a hawk followed it right into his oratory, and the one who had come at the usual time to capture his meal was himself captured, and became his own captor's prey and food.

But then, although Bartholomew was absent in body, he was present in power, for when the hawk who had done him the injury wanted to get out, it was unable to do so. Its wings bore it recklessly hither and thither. Again and again it dashed itself at the window and was driven back as if from a wall. At the open door, too, it found a solid barrier. At last, weary and worn out, it happened to land just above the place where the renowned father was accustomed to sit down.

So when Bartholomew returned from fishing and discovered in the confines of his oratory the little feathers and bones, he realised that they were the remains of his pet bird and he was greatly grieved. When he had sat down for a little while he raised his eyes and saw the killer of his bird, still showing the fresh signs of blood on its beak and talons. 'You wretched creature,' he said to it, 'Have you been so presumptuous as to attack our bird in this rash venture?' And seizing it with both hands he shut it up for two days so that it might purge the guilt of such villainy by fasting; but on the third day, moved by mercy, he let it go.

Bartholomew to the Rescue

From the most ancient times the island of Farne has been inhabited by certain birds whose name and species miraculously continue. They gather here at nesting-time, and so great is the grace of gentleness which they thereafter receive from the holiness of the place—or rather from those who have made it holy by their way of life—that they do not shrink from human contact and gaze. They love quietness and yet are not disturbed by any noise. They make their nests everywhere, far from the inhabitants. Some sit on their eggs by the side of the altar. No-one presumes to hurt them or touch their eggs without permission. As soon as their ducklings are born, they follow behind their mothers, who lead the way, and once they enter their native waves they do not return to their nests.

It happened at one time, when a mother was going in front of her ducklings and leading the way, that one of them fell down a deep crevice in the fissured cliff. The mother stood by in great distress, and no-one could doubt that at that moment she had assumed human reason. For she immediately turned round, left her young behind her, came to Bartholomew and began tugging at the hem of his robe with her beak as if to say plainly: 'Get up and follow me, and give me back my child.' Bartholomew got up at once, for he thought she was looking underneath him for her nest. But when she tugged more and more, he realised that she was asking something which she did not know how to explain in any spoken way: she was as skilled in actions as she was unskilled in words. She led the way, therefore, and he followed her; and when they came to the cliff she pointed out the place with her beak. Looking intently at Bartholomew, she indicated with whatever signs she could that he should look down into it. He went closer and saw the duckling clinging to the cliff with its little wings: down he climbed, and brought it back to its mother. She was highly delighted and, with a look full of joy, seemed to thank him. Then she went into the water with her young, and Bartholomew, utterly astonished, returned to his oratory.

BENEDICT OF NURSIA

Benedict's Raven

[As a consequence of Benedict's holiness and the miracles he performed, his fame spread rapidly around the monastery at Vicovaro, and before long he had founded a chain of twelve monasteries, each with an abbot and twelve monks. But in a church nearby there lived a priest called Florentius who was deeply envious of Benedict and determined to do all that he could to damage his reputation. But the more he tried to disparage the saint, the greater grew his renown, and this, naturally, infuriated Florentius all the more. At last, he became so insanely jealous of Benedict that he determined to move from malice to murder, and after inserting a deadly poison into a loaf of bread, he sent it to Benedict *quasi pro benedictione.* Benedict accepted the gift and thanked him, but he was well aware that there was poison concealed within it. Gregory the Great now takes up the story:]

There was a raven which used to come from the nearby woods at meal-times and take bread from the saint's hand; and when it had arrived, in accor-dance with its usual custom, the man of God took the bread which the priest had sent him, put it in front of the raven, and gave it this instruction: 'In the name of Jesus Christ our Lord, take this bread and drop it in some place where no-one can find it.' Then the raven opened its mouth and spread its wings and began to caw and circle round the bread as if to say clearly that it wanted to obey, and yet found it impossible to fulfil the saint's command. Again and again the man of the Lord said to it: 'Pick it up, pick it up! It's quite safe! And then drop it where it can't be found.' So after much hesitation, the raven eventually picked it up in its beak and flew away. Some three hours later, when it had thrown away the bread, it came back and received its usual meal from the hand of the man of God.

[Florentius, however, was not to be thwarted; and realising that Benedict himself was immune to his attacks, he decided to assail his monks instead. He therefore sent seven naked girls into the garden of Benedict's monastery with instructions to dance as lewdly and lasciviously as possible and thereby lure the younger monks into sin. Benedict, however, refused to do battle with Florentius and decided to leave the monastery and settle elsewhere. But soon after he had left, the omnipotent God struck down Florentius with a terrible vengeance: as he was standing in the sun on his balcony, pondering on these events and congratulating himself, the entire structure collapsed and crushed him to death.]

BENNO OF MEISSEN

Frogsong

The man of God would often go about the fields praying and meditating; and when, on some occasion, he was near a marsh, a talkative frog was croaking away in the muddy water. So to prevent it disturbing his contemplation, he commanded it to be a Seraphian, since all the frogs in Seraphus are dumb. But when he had gone on a little further, he called to mind this verse in Daniel: 'Bless the Lord, you whales and all that move in the waters; bless the Lord, all you beasts and cattle' (Dan 3: 79, 81). So fearing that the frogs' song might be

more pleasing to God than his own prayer, he gave them another command: that they praise God in their usual way. And
very soon the fields and the air were filled with their strident
conversation.

BERNARD OF CLAIRVAUX

The Flies of Foigny

At one time Bernard went to Foigny, one
of the first abbeys he built, which is located in the
diocese of Laon. When everything was being made
ready for the dedication of the new church there,
it was infested by an incredible swarm of flies;
and their buzzing and ceaseless flying about was
a very great nuisance to those coming in. Since
there was no remedy for it, the saint said: 'I ex-
communicate them!' And next morning every one
of them was dead. Since they covered the whole
floor, they shovelled them outside with spades,
and in this way the basilica was finally cleansed.
So well known and so celebrated was this event
that among those living nearby—and a great crowd of them
had come to the dedication—the cursing of the flies of Foigny
became proverbial.

How to Catch a Horse

[On another occasion, when Bernard and other brothers were returning from Châlons-sur-Marne, it was very cold
and windy, and the whole company was suffering from the
inclement weather. Most of Bernard's escort pressed on ahead,

paying little attention to the saint because they were so cold, and Bernard ended up following along after them almost on his own. William of Saint-Thierry now takes up the tale:] Two alone remained with him, but one of these carelessly let his horse go and it escaped, running about on the open plain. When they were unable to catch it, and the wild weather prevented them from spending any longer on the matter, Bernard said: 'Let us pray.' He then knelt in prayer with the one brother who was with him, and they were hardly able to finish the Lord's Prayer when lo! the horse came back as tame as could be, stood at Bernard's feet, and was restored to its rider.

BLAISE

The Miracles of Saint Blaise

Blaise was so esteemed for his great gentleness and holiness that the Christians of the city of Sebaste in Cappadocia chose him as their bishop. But because of the persecution of Diocletian, he sought out a cave after he had received the episcopate and there led the life of a hermit. The birds used to bring him food, and after flying to him all together as they usually did, they would refuse to leave him until he had laid his hand upon them in blessing. People who were sick would also come to him without delay and have their health fully restored.

It happened once that the governor of the area sent his soldiers out to hunt, but after they had laboured there to no avail, they chanced upon the cave of Saint Blaise. There they found a great crowd of animals standing before him, but there was no way in which they could capture any of them. They were amazed at this, and when they reported it to their master he immediately sent a number of soldiers with orders to bring Blaise to him, together with all the other Christians. But that very night Christ appeared to him three times and said: 'Arise, and offer sacrifice to me.'

The soldiers then arrived and said: 'Come out! The governor has summoned you!' 'You are welcome, my sons', said Saint Blaise, 'I see now that God has not forgotten me.' He went off with them and preached continually, and performed many miracles in their presence.

There was a woman who had a son who was dying—he had a fish-bone stuck sideways in his throat—and she brought him to the feet of Saint Blaise and tearfully implored him to heal him. Saint Blaise laid his hand upon him and prayed that this boy, and all those who asked anything in his name, might obtain the benefit of health, and he was immediately healed.

There was another poor woman who had a single pig, but a wolf had seized it and carried it off. She entreated Saint Blaise to have her pig restored to her. He smiled and said: 'Don't be sad, woman; your pig has come back to you.' And there and then the wolf came up and brought back the widow's pig.

BRENDAN THE VOYAGER

Iasconius

When they arrived at another island, the boat came to a standstill before they could reach the landing-place. Saint Brendan commanded the brothers to get out of the boat into

the sea, and this they did. They then pulled the boat along
with ropes on both sides until they came to the landing-place.
The island was stony and grassless; there were a few bushes
there, but there was no sand on the shore. While the brothers spent the night in the open, praying and keeping watch,
the man of God sat inside in the boat. He knew what kind of
island it was, but he did not want to tell the others lest they
should be terrified.

When morning came, he told each of the priests to sing
Mass, and this they did. While Saint Brendan himself was also
singing Mass in the boat, the brothers began to bring from the
boat the raw meat and fish which they had brought with them
from another island so that they could salt it and preserve it.
When they had done this, they set a cooking-pot on a fire; but
when they were feeding the fire with sticks and the pot began
to boil, the island started to heave, just like a wave!

The brothers ran for the boat, imploring their holy
father for protection. He took their hands and pulled them
into the boat one by one, and they began to sail away, leaving
behind them on the island everything they had brought with
them. The island then moved out to sea, and the flames of the
fire could still be seen more than two miles away.

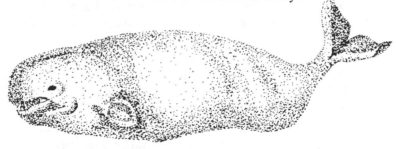

Then Saint Brendan told the brothers what it really
was, saying: 'Are you surprised, brothers, at the behaviour of
this island?' 'Indeed we are surprised,' they said, 'and not a
little terrified!' He said to them: 'My little children, do not be
afraid. During the night God revealed to me in a vision the

mystery of this business. Where we were was not an island, but a fish—the first of all who swim in the ocean. He is ever seeking to bring his tail round to meet his head, but because of his length he cannot do it. His name is Iasconius.'

The True Nature of Birds

[They then sailed on to another island, a lush place with groves of trees, rich grass, and a profusion of flowers. They circled it, looking for a place to land, and discovered a river flowing down to the sea. The brothers then got out of the boat, attached ropes to the sides, and hauled it about a mile up the river to the spring at its source. Here Saint Brendan decided to stay for a time while he and the brothers celebrated Easter.]
Over the spring there stood a tree of astonishing size, both in girth and in height, and it was covered with the whitest of white birds. They covered so much of it that one could scarcely see the leaves or the branches. When the man of God saw this he began to think and ponder to himself what this might be and what could be the reason for such a huge flock of birds to be gathered together. He was so irked by this that tears poured forth and flowed down his cheeks, and he besought God, saying: 'O God, knower of the unknown and revealer of all secrets, you know how anxious is my heart! I beseech your majesty, through your great mercy, to deign to reveal to me, a sinner, this secret of yours which now I see before my eyes. It is not through my merits or my worth that I presume to ask, but through your boundless clemency.'
When he had said this within himself and had sat down again, one of the birds flew down from the tree—her wings making a noise like a hand-bell—and came to the boat where the man of God was sitting. She alighted on the point of the prow and began to stretch her wings, as if indicating

her happiness, and gazed placidly at the holy father. The man of God realised immediately that God had heard his plea and said to the bird: 'If you are a messenger of God, tell me where these birds come from and why they are gathered together here.'

She said at once: 'We are from the great ruin of the Ancient Enemy, but we did not join with them in sinning. But when we were created, the fall of the Enemy and his followers also brought about our ruin. Our God, however, is just and true, and through his great judgment, he sent us to this place. We suffer no pain here and we see the presence of God; but he has still separated us from sharing the lot of those who stood faithful. We wander through the different parts of the air and the heavens and the earth, as do the other spirits who are sent forth. But on holy days and Sundays we receive such bodies as now you see so that we may stay here and praise our Creator. You and your brothers have now been on your journey for one year. Six more remain. Where you celebrate Easter today, there you will celebrate it every year; and after that you will find what you have held in your heart: the Promised Land of the Saints.'

Having said this, the bird lifted herself off the prow and flew back to the others.

A Diet of Fish

[Much later, and many leagues further on, Brendan and his band of brothers arrived at yet another island, but were this time plunged into the gravest danger:]

They then sailed to another island, small but very lovely, where there was to be seen a deep pool in which, from ancient times, fish could be caught. The creatures of the sea used to be stranded there when the tide went out. When they

crossed the island, they found a stone church where a venerable old man was praying. What did I say? An old man? They
saw hardly more than
animated bones! And
this old man said to
them: 'Holy men of
God, flee from this
island as fast as you
can! There is a cat here
of great age, a most
crafty animal, which
has grown huge from eating quantities of fish!' So they hurried
quickly back to their boat and left the island.

But they then saw behind them the beast swimming
through the sea, and its great eyes were like the bottoms of
glass bottles. All of them immediately started to pray, but
Brendan said: 'Lord Jesus Christ, keep back your beast!'
Straightaway there rose up from the deep sea another beast
which swam up to the first and fought it, and both of them
sank down into the depths of the sea. Nor was either of them
ever seen again. Then they thanked God and returned to the
old man to ask him who he was and where he came from.

'There were twelve men,' he said, 'who came to this
place from the island of Ireland, seeking the place of our resurrection. Eleven are dead, and I alone remain, O saint of God,
awaiting the Sacrifice of the Mass from your hands. We
brought with us in the ship a cat which was most affectionate
towards us, but as I told you earlier, he grew huge from eating
so much fish. Nevertheless, our Lord Jesus Christ did not permit him to harm us.' He then pointed out to them the way to
the land they were looking for, and after receiving the Sacrifice
of the Mass from the hands of Brendan, he happily fell asleep
in the Lord. They buried him there among his companions.

BRYNACH

The Wolf and the Resurrected Cow

The Lord so glorified Brynach in peoples' sight that he made the wild beasts put aside their savage ways and become tame at his command. So whenever he wanted to go from dwelling to dwelling, he would call two stags from the herd and bid them pull a cart in which were placed whatever household things needed to be moved. When they were unyoked, they would go back to their usual pastures.

There was also a cow which he had set apart from the others as if she were unique and exactly right for his needs, both because of her physical size (she was bigger than the rest) and because she gave so much milk. He gave her into the charge of a wolf who, like a well-trained herdsman, would lead the cow to pasture in the morning and bring her safely home again in the evening.

It happened at that time that Maelgwyn, the king of Wales, was on a journey not far from the saint's cell and he sent him a message ordering him to prepare a meal for him. But the saint, who wanted himself, his dependents, and, in addition, his monastic foundations, to be free from any obligation, stated that he owed no meal to the king, nor was he at all willing to obey his unjust command. Those who had been sent returned to their master and told him that the man to whom he had sent the message was not in any way willing to prepare a meal for him. The king, however, was very short tempered and was known to be quicker to harm than hasty to help; he gave no thought to piety, none to holiness, and none to modesty. He therefore sent his attendants to fetch the saint's cow and prepare his meal from her; nor, undoubtedly, would he have spared the others except that they were kept in pastures far away. In his fury he heaped threat upon threat, saying that on the very next day he would banish the saint from his kingdom and utterly raze his monastic foundations to the ground.

The agents of iniquity run off and quickly fetch the cow. They prepare their prey, and for the coming meal they tear the hide away from the ribs and expose the entrails. Part of it they cut in pieces and put in a cauldron on the fire. They feed the fire with wood and on all sides they quickly puff out their cheeks and blow on the flames. Meanwhile, the wolf, the cow's guardian, runs to its master and lies prostrate on the ground, sad and sighing, as if it were going to ask for forgiveness. But there was someone there who was able to tell Brynach that the servants of the king had carried off the cow, cut it into pieces, and laid it out to be cooked. The saint then placed his grievance before God and gave over the whole matter to be aired by the divine will.

The king and his household are tormented with hunger, but as yet they are given no hope of a meal. Indeed, the water into which they had put the flesh for cooking remained just as cold as it was when it was first poured in! And when they put beneath it a fire beyond all compare, it was no more inclined to boil than if they had taken the fire away and substituted for it a great lump of ice!

The king and his men felt the power of God and realised that the saint was at work. They had heard earlier that he was precious to God and now they were transfixed with

sheer terror. Maelgwyn was immediately humbled and put aside his kingly arrogance, and all his men were equally contrite: with bare feet they stepped forward and came to the saint. They all prostrated themselves on the ground at his feet and the king, who, on the advice of his men, acted as their spokesman, confessed that both he and his men had sinned against him and promised that he would not do such things again. With humble prayer and sincere devotion he begged the saint to have pity on him and to pray to the Almighty for him and his associates. Saint Brynach, who was wholly without bitterness, prayed to his Lord, took the king's right hand, raised him up, and gave him confidence and hope in the kindness of the Most High. Then, in the sight of all, he restored the cow to her former state and gave her once more into the care of the wolf.

BUITE

Reparation

One day, when the brothers had gone out on the business of the monastery and the blessed man was sitting alone in the cloister, a wolf came in, killed the calf of the brothers' only cow and ate it. There was an outcry and an uproar in the monastery; and when he heard it, the holy man went out to find the reason for the racket.

In the meantime the wolf, leaping over the palisade, had been pierced in the foot by a stake: in this way it was miraculously restrained as a punishment, for it could neither flee nor even move. The venerable father hastened up to give help to the wolf in its need, and when the wolf saw him it put aside its fierceness, flattened its ears, and, although unused to it, showed all the signs of tameness. But the venerable father, rendering good for evil, gently pulled out the stake from the wolf's foot, made the sign of the cross on the wound, and immediately restored it to health.

Thereupon the wolf headed for the woods and, a short time later, brought back a fawn and presented it to the man of God. He signed it with the sign of the cross and, from being wild, it became tame; and the calfless cow cherished it as her own calf.

CANICE

The Isle of Birds

One Sunday, Saint Canice was staying on an island called the Isle of Birds. But the birds there were garrulous and very talkative and annoyed the saint of God. He therefore forbade their chattering and they obeyed his command: all the birds gathered together, their breasts to the ground, and were silent. And there they remained, quiet and motionless, until Matins on Monday when the holy man, by his word, released them.

The Runaway Lectern

On another occasion, when Saint Canice was hidden away in solitude, a stag came to him there and would carefully hold on its antlers whatever book the saint was reading. One day, however, something startled it, and without its abbot's permission, it erupted in flight with the open book still supported on its antlers. But then, with the book in the same position, safe and sound on its antlers, it returned to Saint Canice like a fugitive monk to his abbot.

CARANNOG

Saint Carannog and the Dragon

In those times Cadwy and Arthur were reigning in that part of the country and were residing at Dindraithou. And Arthur came to Carhampton looking for a dragon of the greatest strength, huge and terrible, which had laid waste twelve portions of the lands in the area. Carannog came and greeted Arthur who gladly received a blessing from him. Carannog then asked Arthur if he had heard where his altar had come to shore, and Arthur replied: 'I will tell you, provided I get a reward for doing so.' 'What reward do you want?', asked Carannog. 'The dragon I am looking for is here in your neighbourhood,' Arthur said, 'If you are a servant of God, summon it here so that we can see it.'

Then the blessed Carannog went and prayed to the Lord, and there and then, like a calf running to its mother, the dragon came up with a great roaring. It bowed its head before the servant of God like a servant obeying its master, its heart humble and its eyes docile. Carannog placed his stole around its neck and led it like a lamb, nor did it extend its wings or talons. Its neck was like the neck of a seven year old bull and the stole would scarcely go round it.

They then went to the citadel, greeted Cadwy, and were well received by him. And Carannog led the dragon into the centre of the hall and there, in front of the people, he fed it. They, however, tried to kill it, but this he would not permit them to do. It had come at God's command, he said, to destroy the sinners in Carhampton and through it to show forth

the power of God. After this, Carannog went outside the gate of the citadel and released the dragon, and commanded it to go away and harm no one, and never again to return. Off it went and remained in the neighbourhood as the ordinance of God had earlier decreed. Carannog then took back the altar which Arthur had intended making into a table, except that whatever was placed upon it was hurled far away. Then the king asked Carannog to accept Carhampton for ever by a written deed, and afterwards he built a church there.

CIARAN OF CLONMACNOISE

The Hungry Wolf

One day, when Saint Ciaran was guarding the cattle, a cow gave birth to a calf in front of him. At that very moment the godly boy saw a wolf coming towards him, wretched and weak and hungry, and the servant of God said to him: 'Come here, you poor creature, and eat this calf.' And the wolf devoured it.

When the holy herdsman came home with his cattle, the cow was looking for her calf and mooing loudly. When she saw this, Derercha, Saint Ciaran's mother, said to him: 'Ciaran, where is this cow's calf? Bring it back, whether from the sea or from the earth. It is you who have lost it and its mother is very sad at heart.'

Hearing these words, Saint Ciaran went back to the place where the wolf had devoured the calf and gathered up its bones into the front of his tunic; and when he arrived back, he laid them down in front of the grieving cow. And straight-away, because of the boy's holiness, the calf was restored to life by divine power in the sight of all; and it stood on its feet, healthy and whole, playing with its mother.

CIARAN OF SAIGHIR

The First Monks at Fuaran

[After thirty years in Ireland, Ciaran decided to go
to Rome where he was baptised and where he remained for
a further twenty years. There he met Saint Patrick who told
him to return to Ireland and make his way to Fuaran, on the
border of Northern and Southern Ireland, and there found a
monastery. Ciaran did this and it is when he had first arrived
at Fuaran that the following events took place:]

When Saint Ciaran first arrived there he was sitting
under a tree, and in the shadow of the tree was a most ferocious boar. As soon as the boar saw the man, it fled in utter
terror; but then, rendered tame by God, it came back to the
holy man as if it were a servant. That boar was Saint Ciaran's
first disciple or monk, so to speak, in that place. Straightaway,
in the sight of the man of God, the boar used its teeth and its
strength to cut twigs and grass as materials for building a little
cell, for until that time there was no-one there with the saint of
God. He had eluded his disciples and come to that wild place
alone. But later on, other animals came from their dens in the
wild to the holy Ciaran—a fox and a badger and a wolf and a
doe—and they stayed with him, completely tame. They used
to obey the commands of the holy man in all things, just as if
they were his monks.

The Fox and His Abbot's Shoes

On another day a fox, who was more crafty and cunning than the other animals, stole the shoes of his abbot (that is to say, of Saint Ciaran) and abandoning his vow, took them to his old den in the forest intending to eat them there. Knowing this, the holy father Ciaran sent another monk or brother—that is, the badger—into the forest after the fox to bring back the brother to his place.

The badger, who was familiar with the woods, obeyed the command of the old man and set off at once. He made his way straight to the cave of Brother Fox and found him there about to eat his master's shoes. He bit his two ears and his tail, tore out some of his hair, and forced him to come back with him to his monastery so that he could do penance there for his theft. So the fox, with no choice in the matter, together with the badger, who had the saint's uneaten shoes, arrived at the cell of Saint Ciaran at None.

The holy man said to the fox: 'Brother, why did you do this wicked deed which monks should not do? See, our water is sweet and for everyone's use and the food is likewise shared in common among us all. And if you had wanted to eat some meat, which for you is only natural, then for our sake Almighty God would have made it for you from the bark of the trees.' Then the fox begged his forgiveness, did penance by fasting, and would not eat again until he was commanded to do so by the holy man. Thereafter he remained with the others as one of the family.

In course of time his own disciples and many others gathered to Saint Ciaran in that place from all parts, and this was the beginning of a famous monastery. But the tame animals we have been talking about lived there all their lives, for the holy man was always pleased to see them.

COLUMBA OF IONA

The Loch Ness Monster

On one occasion, when the blessed Columba was delayed for a few days in the country of the Picts, he had to cross the River Ness. When he arrived at its bank he saw a poor creature being buried by others who lived nearby. Those who were burying him said that a short while ago he had been swimming and that a beast which lived in the water had seized him and bitten him with the utmost savagery. Some others had gone out in a wooden boat but they were too late, and they had dragged out his wretched corpse with grappling hooks.

Nevertheless, when the blessed Columba heard this, he ordered one of his companions to swim over and sail back to him in a boat which was lying on the opposite bank. When he heard the command of the praiseworthy Columba, Lugne MacMin obeyed without the slightest hesitation: he stripped off all his clothes except his tunic and dived into the water. But deep in the river lurked the monster, who had not been sated earlier, but whose desire for prey had instead been increased. When it felt the water above it being disturbed by Lugne's swimming, it suddenly swam up and surfaced, and with wide-open mouth and a mighty roaring, rushed towards the man swimming in the middle of the river.

Everyone there, the barbarians and even the brothers, were wholly terrified, but when the blessed Columba saw what was happening, he raised his holy hand and drew the saving sign of the cross in the empty air. Invoking the name of God, he commanded the ferocious beast saying: 'Go no further and do not touch this man! Go back again immediately!' When it heard the saint's voice, the beast, as if pulled back by ropes, fled in terror and retreated as quickly as possible. But it had previously come so close to Lugne as he swam that between man and beast there was no more than about fifteen feet.

When the brothers saw that the beast had gone and that Lugne, their fellow-soldier, had returned to them in the boat safe and sound, they were utterly astonished and glorified God in the blessed Columba. But the pagan barbarians who were there at the time, incited by the magnitude of the miracle they too had witnessed, also magnified the God of the Christians.

The Consequences of Disobedience

One day, when the venerable Columba was staying on the island of Iona, one of the brothers, whose name was Berach, was intending to sail to the island of Tiree. In the morning he went to the saint and asked for his blessing. The saint looked at him and said: 'My son, today you must be very careful not to take the direct route straight across the open sea to Tiree. Sail round by the little islands instead; otherwise you will be terrified by an enormous monster and scarcely able to make your escape.'

After he had received the saint's blessing, Berach went away and boarded his ship, and then, as if belittling the saint's instruction, he transgressed it. So when he and the sailors with him were crossing the great stretch of sea to Tiree, they looked up and there was a whale of vast and wondrous size which rose up like a mountain, and swimming on the surface, opened wide a mouth bristling with teeth. The rowers, wholly terrified, lowered the sail and reversed their course, and were just able to escape from the wash raised by the monster's motion. Then, remembering the saint's prophecy, they were amazed.

On the morning of the very same day the saint told Baithene, who was also going to sail to the island we have just mentioned, about the same whale and said: 'In the middle of last night a great whale came up from the ocean depths and today it will come to the surface of the sea between the islands of Iona and Tiree.' Baithene replied: 'Both I and that monster are under the power of God.' 'Go in peace,' said Columba, 'your faith in Christ will protect you from this danger.'

Baithene then received the saint's blessing and sailed out of the harbour. After crossing no small stretch of sea he and his companions saw the whale, and while all of them were terrified, Baithene raised his hands and calmly blessed both the sea and the whale. Straightaway the great beast submerged beneath the waves and never appeared to them again.

Hospitality

At another time, when the saint was living on the island of Iona, he called one of the brothers and gave him these instructions: 'Three days from now, at dawn, go to the western part of this island, sit above the sea-shore and wait. When the third hour before sunset has passed, a guest will arrive from the northern region of Ireland, a crane which has been tossed about by the winds and driven hither and thither through vast reaches of air. She will be very tired and weary, her strength almost gone, and she will fall at your feet and lie on the shore. Be careful to lift her up tenderly and carry her to the house nearby; take her in as a guest and for three days and nights look after her and feed her with proper care. Afterwards, when the three days are up, she will be revived, and then, not wishing to spend more time with us in her pilgrimage, she will go back to the old, sweet land of Ireland whence she came, her

strength fully restored. The reason I commend her to you so
earnestly is because she comes from the land of our fathers.'

The brother obeyed, and on the third day, just after the
third hour before sunset, he awaited the arrival of the foretold
guest, as he had been bidden. When she arrived he lifted her
from the shore where she had fallen, carried her, weak as she
was, to the lodging, and since she was hungry, he fed her.
When he returned to the monastery that evening, the saint
did not question him about these things, but confirmed them,
saying: 'God bless you,
my son, since you have
looked after this pilgrim
guest so well. She will not
tarry in her pilgrimage, but
after three days she will go
back home.'

Things occurred
exactly as the saint had
foretold: after staying as
a guest for three days, she
first soared from earth high
into the sky in the presence of her host who had looked after
her, and after a short while, spying out her way in the air, she
crossed the ocean sea and, in calm weather, flew straight back
to Ireland.

The Sorrow of Columba's Horse

[On the last day of his life, Columba went with an
attendant to bless one of the monastery barns, but was aware
that he would die that night. 'Now my Lord Jesus has seen
fit to invite me,' he said. 'To him, I say, and at his invitation I
shall depart at midnight tonight. Thus it has been revealed to
me by the Lord himself.' Adomnan now takes up the story:]

After this, the saint left the barn and halfway back to the monastery sat down to rest. On that spot a cross was later set in a mill-stone and you can still see it there today by the side of the road. While the saint was sitting there resting for a little while—he was weary with age, as I have said—there came up to him a white horse, his obedient servant who used to carry the milk pails between the cow-pasture and the monastery. He came up to the saint and (marvellous to relate!) leaned his head on his breast. I believe he was inspired by God (for to him every creature has understanding in whatever way the Creator has decreed) and knew that his master would soon be departing and that he would see him no more. He began to mourn,  and his tears, like those of a human being, flowed down in abundance into the saint's lap, and foaming at the mouth, he wept aloud.

When the saint's servant saw this, he started to drive away the weeping mourner, but the saint forbade him, saying: 'Let him be! Let him be! Let this one who loves us pour out his tears of bitter sorrow here on my breast. You see, there was no way that you, man though you are with a rational soul, could have known anything about my departure save what I have just revealed to you, but to this beast, this irrational animal, the Creator, in whatever way he would, clearly revealed that its master is about to depart from it.' So saying, he blessed the sad horse who had served him as it turned away from him.

CUTHBERT OF LINDISFARNE

An Equine Provider

[One day, when Cuthbert was making one of his missionary journeys from Melrose, he arrived at a distant village and went to one of the houses to rest there a while and ask for food, not for himself, but for the horse he was riding. The housewife received him kindly, but when she asked if she might prepare a meal for him, he refused because it was a Friday, a day 'on which most of the faithful are accustomed to extend their fast until three o'clock in the afternoon out of reverence for the Lord's Passion'. And although the woman persisted in her entreaties and explained to Cuthbert that he would not reach any other village before sunset, the saint refused to eat, mounted his horse, and set off again on his journey. Bede now takes up the tale:]

But when evening was at hand, he realised that it was impossible for him to finish the journey he had proposed on the same day and that there were no lodgings in the neighbourhood where he could stay. Then suddenly, while he was travelling, he saw some shepherds' huts nearby which had been roughly built during the summer and which were now standing open and empty. He went into one of them to pass the night, tethered the horse on which he had come to the wall, collected a bundle of hay which the wind had brought down from the roof, and gave it to the horse to eat. He himself began to spend the time in prayer.

Suddenly, while he was singing psalms, he saw the horse lift up its head, seize the straw roof of the hut in its mouth and bring it down. In among the straw falling from the roof there also fell a folded cloth, and since he wanted to find out for certain what it might be, he went up to it after finishing his prayer and found, folded up in the cloth, half a loaf of bread, still warm, and some meat, enough for one meal for himself. Then, singing praise for the heavenly favours, he said: 'Thanks be to God who has seen fit to provide dinner both for me, who am fasting for love of him, and for my companion'. He therefore broke in two the piece of bread that he had found, gave half to his horse, and kept the rest for his own  food. From that day on he became more ready to fast, since he knew for certain that he had been provided with food in his solitude by the gift of Him who, by means of the birds and for no short time, had once fed Elijah in solitude with the same sort of food because there were no people there to attend him.

These things a priest called Ingwald, a monk of our monastery at the mouth of the River Wear, told me he had heard from Cuthbert himself, who was then a bishop.

What the Brother Saw

It was Cuthbert's usual custom to go out and pray alone while the others were sleeping at night, and then, after long vigils in the dead of night, he would return home just in time for communal worship. One night, one of the brothers from the monastery saw him go out silently, and since he wanted to find out where he went and what he meant to do, he secretly followed in his footsteps. With the spy following, Cuthbert left the monastery and went down to the sea, above whose shores the monastery of Melrose was built. He went into the deep sea until the swelling waters rose as high as his neck and arms, and passed the darkness of the night wide awake in praise, accompanied by the sound of the sea. When dawn was at hand, he went back onto the land and there, kneeling on the shore, began again to pray.

While he was doing this, there immediately came up from the depths of the sea two four-footed animals which are commonly called otters. They stretched themselves out in front of him on the sand and began to warm his feet with their

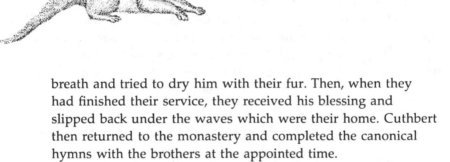

breath and tried to dry him with their fur. Then, when they had finished their service, they received his blessing and slipped back under the waves which were their home. Cuthbert then returned to the monastery and completed the canonical hymns with the brothers at the appointed time.

But the brother who had been waiting for him on the cliffs was struck with such deadly fear and consumed by such anxiety that his tottering steps could scarcely take him home. Early in the morning he came to Cuthbert, prostrated himself on the ground and, in tears, begged his forgiveness for the guilt of his foolish adventure, never doubting that Cuthbert knew what he had done that night and why he was suffering. 'What is it, brother?', said Cuthbert. 'What have you done? Have you been tempted to spy on my nightly journey? Well, I will pardon your offence on one condition: you must promise me that before my death you will tell no-one what you have seen'. So when the brother had given his promise, he blessed him, and freed him both from the fault and from the worry he had so recklessly incurred. So long as Cuthbert was alive, the brother kept silent about the wonder he had seen; but after his death he took pains to tell it to many.

The Worker Is Worthy of Her Hire

[It happened one day that Cuthbert had left the monastery at Melrose to go preaching. He was accompanied this time by a young servant, and although they had been travelling for many hours there was still a long way to go before they could reach their destination. Cuthbert then asked the lad who was with him where he intended to eat and whether he knew anyone on the way. 'I've been thinking a lot about that', said the boy, and went on to say that he knew no-one at all with whom they could stay, that they had brought no food with them, and that he could not see how they could reach the end of their journey without a considerable amount of suffering. Then, says Bede:]

The man of God said: 'Dear son, learn to have faith and hope in the Lord always, for no-one who serves God faithfully will die from hunger.' And looking up, he saw an eagle flying in the sky. 'Do you see that eagle flying far off?', he said. 'It is possible for God to refresh us today even through her ministry.'

Talking in this way they continued their journey along a certain river when all of a sudden they see the eagle settling on the bank. The man of God said: 'Do you see where our handmaid is settling, the one I told you about earlier? Run, I beg you, and see what sort of meal she has brought us from the Lord, and bring it here as soon as you can.' The boy ran off and brought back a large fish which the eagle had just snatched from the river. But the man of God said: 'What have you done, my son? Why haven't you given our handmaid

her share? Cut it in half as quickly as you can and take her
the share she deserves for ministering to us.' The lad did as
he was told and kept back the other half. When it was time
for their meal, they turned aside at the next village. There they
handed over the piece of fish to be broiled and refreshed both
themselves and those into whose house they had entered with
a most welcome meal. Cuthbert preached the word of God
and praised him for his bounty, and they then resumed their
journey to those they had set out intending to teach.

The Birds and the Barley

[When Cuthbert first went to live on Inner Farne he
would eat bread brought to him by visitors and drink water
from his own well. But after a while he decided that he should
emulate the early fathers and live by the labour of his own
hands. The wheat he planted, however, failed to germinate
(Cuthbert was not quite sure whether this was the result of
God's will or the climate), but when he turned to barley, the

results were excellent and the crop abundant. This, unfortunately, delighted not only Cuthbert but also the local avian population, and, as Bede tells us:]

When the crop had begun to ripen, the birds came and avidly set about devouring it. Then, as he himself used to tell us afterwards, the most devout servant of Christ went up to them and said: 'Why do you meddle with crops you did not sow? Or is it that you have more need of them than I? If you have had God's permission, then do what he has allowed you to do; but if not, then off with you, and don't damage other people's property again!' When he said this, the whole flock flew away at the first sound of his voice, and never again attacked his harvest.

The Penitent Ravens

It is a pleasure to tell of a miracle performed by blessed Cuthbert after the example of father Benedict, in which human wilfulness and pride were openly condemned by the obedience and humility of birds.

There were some ravens who had been living on Farne Island for a long time. One day, when they were building their nests, the man of God spotted them tearing with their beaks at the little guest-house of the brothers and carrying away in their bills bits of the thatch which made up its roof to make their own nests. He restrained them with a slight gesture of his right hand and ordered them to stop injuring the brothers. But when they scorned his command, he said: 'In the name of Jesus Christ, go away at once, and do not presume to stay any longer in the place you are damaging!' He had hardly finished his words when sadly, but without delay, they all went away.

After three days had passed, one of a pair returned and found the servant of Christ digging. Then, with its feathers lamentably ruffled and its head bowed down to its feet, with humble caws and using whatever signs it could, it begged

forgiveness. The venerable father understood this and gave
it permission to come back, and once it had been given leave
to return it soon went off to bring back its mate. Both of them
returned without
delay and brought
with them a wor-
thy gift: a lump
of hog's lard. Of-
ten afterwards the
man of God would
show this to the
brothers who came
to see him and

offer it to them to grease their shoes. He thereby showed them
what care people should take to possess obedience and humility since even the proudest of birds, with prayers, lamentations,
and gifts, was quick to cleanse itself of the injury it had offered
to the man of God. Finally, to provide people with an example
of reform, the birds stayed for many years on that island and
built their nests, but they did not dare to inflict any trouble
on anyone.

ELIJAH B. SOLOMON,
THE GAON OF WILNA

The Gifts of the Animals

God (blessed be He!)
turned to the animals he had made
and spoke these words: 'Let us
make a human being: together, in
partnership, we shall make a

human being. Each one of you creatures shall make a specific contribution: from the cat he shall derive modesty; from the ant, honesty; from the tiger, courage; from the lion, strength; from the eagle, alertness; and so forth.'

FIRMINUS

Under the Yoke

When the body of the blessed Firminus, bishop of Uzès and native of Narbonne, was being transported through certain parts of the province to Uzès, it happened that the oxen who were pulling the carriage were unyoked and turned out to pasture. One of them, however, was suddenly devoured by a bear. When he learned of this, Saint Ferreolus, who was Firminus' nephew and the person in charge of the noble procession (and also the immediate successor of Firminus in the episcopal see), straightaway made supplication to God and summoned the bear to him.

As soon as it approached, it willingly submitted to the yoke and devoutly took the place of the dead ox, acting as its substitute in pulling the carriage. Then, when Firminus had been carried the many miles from there to Uzès in this

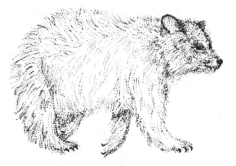

wonderful way, and the funeral rites there had been solemnly and gloriously completed, the bear returned unhurt to the mountains, just as if it had received permission from Ferreolus.

But every year afterwards, for as long

as it lived, the bear was accustomed to come to the church
on the feast of Saint Firminus, lay aside for a while its wild
savagery, and show itself to the people as a tame animal which
could be stroked and handled. It was just as if it were prepared
to undergo the punishment merited by its audacity and the
crime it had committed. And so to this day, its skin is preserved in the church of Saint Firminus and held in veneration,
and it is shown to travellers and pilgrims as a memorial of this
extraordinary miracle.

FLORENTIUS

Florentius and Brother Bear

At one time there lived in the province of Nursia two
men whose lives and actions were both alike holy. One of them
was called Eutychius, the other Florentius. Eutychius grew in
spiritual zeal and fervour and spent much of his time leading
many souls to God with his exhortations; but Florentius led a
life dedicated to simplicity and prayer. There was a monastery
not far away which had lost its superior through death, and
the monks there wanted Eutychius to be in charge of them.
He acceded to their entreaties and governed the monastery for
many years, training the souls of his disciples in the practice of
a holy way of life. But to prevent the oratory in which he had
first lived from being empty, he left there the venerable man
Florentius.

One day, when he was dwelling there alone, Florentius
prostrated himself in prayer and asked almighty God to deign
to send him some comfort while he was living there. And as
soon as he had finished his prayer, he went out of the oratory
and found a bear standing in front of the door. It bowed its
head to the ground and showed no sign of fierceness in its
movements so as to let the man of God understand clearly

that it had come to serve him; and the man of God understood
immediately. And because there were four or five sheep left
at the cell which had no-one to pasture them and guard them,
he gave these instructions to
the bear: 'Go and take these
sheep out to the pasture and
come back again at noon.' This
the bear began to do without a
moment's delay. The role of a
shepherd was thus entrusted to
the bear, and the sheep which
it was accustomed to eat it now
pastured, restraining its own

animal appetites. When the man of God wanted to fast, he
ordered the bear to bring the sheep back at three o'clock; when
he did not wish to do so, it was to be at noon. And in this way
the bear obeyed all the instructions of the man of God, never
returning at three when its orders said noon, and never at noon
when its orders said three.

After this had been going on for a long time, the fame
of it began to spread far and wide in that part of the country.
But wherever the Ancient Enemy sees good people beginning
to be resplendent with glory, he will there, in his envy, drag
down those who are corrupt to their ruin. And so it happened
that four men who were disciples of the venerable Eutychius
were extremely envious of this miracle, for whereas Florentius,
whom Eutychius had left on his own, was famous for it, it was
a wonder which their own master could not do. They therefore
waylaid the bear and killed it.

When the bear did not return at the time he had commanded, Florentius, the man of God, became suspicious, and
after waiting until sunset, he began to lose heart; but the bear
which, in his great simplicity, he used to call 'Brother' never
came back again.

Next day he went to the field to look for both bear and
sheep, and found the former dead. But after making careful
enquiries, he very soon discovered who had killed it. Then he
gave himself up to his grief—weeping more for the malice of

the brothers than for the death of the bear. He was brought to the venerable man Eutychius who tried to comfort him, but there in his presence the man of the Lord, inflamed and goaded by his great sorrow, called down a curse: 'I hope in almighty God', he said, 'that those who killed my bear, a beast who did them no harm, shall now in this life and in the sight of all receive retribution for their malice.'

As soon as he had said this, divine vengeance followed. The four monks who had killed the bear were immediately struck down with the disease of leprosy: their limbs rotted and they died. But once this had happened, the man of God Florentius was utterly terrified and greatly afraid for having cursed the brothers in this way; and so, for the rest of his life, he wept because his prayer had been heard, and he would accuse himself of being cruel and a murderer in bringing about their deaths. We believe that this was done by almighty God to prevent this man of wondrous simplicity from ever again hurling the dart of malediction, however angry or grief-stricken he might be.

FORTUNATUS

Horse Trading

A certain soldier once owned a horse that was mad— so mad that many men together could hardly hold it. Even then it would attack any that it could and savage their limbs with its teeth. So one day, when a number of them had managed to secure it, they led it to Fortunatus, the man of God. He immediately stretched out his hand and made the sign of the cross on its head, and all its madness was changed into gentleness: the animal which had earlier been insane was ever afterwards the most placid of beasts.

When the soldier saw how the power of this miracle had so swiftly changed the madness of the horse, he decided to offer it to the holy man. He, however, refused to accept it; but when the soldier persisted in his entreaties and begged him not to reject his gift, the holy man took a middle course between the two alternatives: on the one hand he would accede to the soldier's request, but on the other, he would refuse to accept the horse as an outright gift for displaying his power. So he first of  all offered the soldier a fair price, and then he accepted the horse which he had been offered. He knew that if he did not take it, the soldier would have been disappointed; and so, compelled by charity, he bought that for which he had no need.

FRANCIS OF ASSISI

The Sermon to the Birds

[Shortly after his conversion, Francis sent Brother Masseo to ask Saint Clare and another friar, Brother Sylvester, what Christ wished him to do. 'That you go through the world preaching,' was the reply, 'for you have not been chosen solely for yourself alone, but also for the salvation of others.' Francis therefore heeded this command and, together with two other brothers, set off on his travels. He first came to Alviano where (according to the *Fioretti*) he established the Third Order 'per universale salute di tutti,' and was then making his way between Cannara and Bevagna when the following events took place:]

As he continued his journey in the same fervour, he looked up and saw a number of trees by the roadside in which there was such a countless throng of birds that Saint Francis was amazed, and said to his companions: 'Wait for me here on the road: I am going to preach to my little sisters the birds.'

He then went into the field and began to preach to the birds that were on the ground, and those that were in the trees immediately came down to him; and the whole assembly stayed there without moving until Saint Francis had finished his sermon. Even then they did not leave until he had given them his blessing. And according  to the later reports of Brother Masseo and Brother Jacopo da Massa, Saint Francis walked among them, his habit brushing up against them, and not a single one stirred. The substance of Saint Francis's sermon was this:

'My little bird sisters, you owe a great deal to God your Creator, and always and everywhere you should praise him because he has given you a twofold and a threefold covering. Then he has given you the freedom to fly anywhere; and he preserved your seed in Noah's ark so that your species would not disappear from the earth. You are also indebted to him for the element of air that he has assigned to you. Besides this, you do not sow and you do not reap, and God feeds you and gives you the rivers and springs for you to drink from. He gives you the mountains and valleys for your refuge and the tall trees in which to make your nests. And because you do not know how to spin or sew, God clothes both you and your little ones. So the Creator loves you very much since he has done so many good things for you. Therefore, my little sisters, beware of the sin of ingratitude, but always strive to praise God.'

While Saint Francis was speaking these words, all those birds began to open their beaks and stretch out their necks, to spread their wings and reverently bow their heads to the ground, and to show with their gestures and their songs that the words of the holy father gave them the greatest delight. Saint Francis himself was glad and rejoiced with them, and was wholly amazed at such a throng of birds, at their beauty and variety, and their attentiveness and familiarity. And for these things he, with them, devoutly praised the Creator.

Finally, when his sermon was finished, Saint Francis made the sign of the cross over them and gave them permission to leave. All those birds then rose up into the air in a single flock with wonderful songs; and then, in accordance with the form of the cross that Saint Francis had made over them, they divided themselves into four groups: one group flew eastward, the second westward, the third southward, and the fourth northward. And each flock sang wonderfully as it went away. In this way they showed that just as Saint Francis, the standard-bearer of the cross of Christ, had preached to them and made the sign of the cross over them, and they, in accordance with this, had divided themselves up and gone singing into the four parts of the world, so the preaching of the cross of Christ, renewed by Saint Francis, was to be carried throughout the whole world by him and his friars—friars who, like birds, possess nothing of their own in this world, but commit their lives to the providence of God alone. To the praise of Christ. Amen.

The Wolf of Gubbio

At the time when Saint Francis was living in the town of Gubbio, there appeared a huge wolf, terrible and fierce, who devoured not only animals, but human beings as well. He was so fierce that all the townspeople were utterly terrified because he would often come close to the town. Whenever anyone went out into the countryside, they went armed, just as if they were going into battle; but even then, no-one who came across the wolf on his own could defend himself against it. And so it came about that through fear of this wolf, no-one dared set foot outside the town.

Because of this, Saint Francis had compassion on the people of the region and determined to go out to this wolf, even though all the townspeople advised him not to. But he made the sign of the holy cross, put all his trust in God, and left the town with his companions. Saint Francis then took the road to the place where the wolf was, although he doubted that the others would go very far. And there and then, in full view of the many townspeople who had come to see this miracle, the said wolf made for Saint Francis with gaping jaws. Saint Francis went towards him, made the sign of the cross, and called to him, saying: 'Come here, Brother Wolf! In the name of Christ I command you to do no harm either to me or to anyone else.' And wonderful to tell! As soon as Saint Francis had made the sign of the cross, the terrible wolf closed his mouth and stopped in his tracks. And when he gave him that command, he came to Saint Francis as gentle as a lamb and lay down at his feet.

Then Saint Francis speaks to him like this: 'Brother Wolf, you have done a great deal of harm in this region, and you have committed the greatest wickedness, destroying and killing God's creatures without his permission. And not only have you killed and eaten the beasts, but you have had the nerve to kill and destroy human beings, made in God's image. For this you deserve the gallows as the worst sort of thief and murderer: everyone is crying out and complaining about you, and this whole region is your enemy. But Brother Wolf, I want to make peace between you and them, so that you shall injure them no more and they shall forgive you all your past offences, and neither people nor dogs will pursue you any longer.'

At these words, the wolf moved his body and tail and ears, and bowed his head, and thereby showed that he

accepted what Saint Francis had said and would observe it. Then Saint Francis said: 'Brother Wolf, since you are pleased to make and to keep this peace, I promise you that for as long as you live I will have the people of this area provide you with a continual supply of food so that you will never again suffer hunger; for I am well aware that you did all this evil because you were hungry. But since I am begging this favour for you, Brother Wolf, I want you to promise me that you will never again injure any person or any animal. Do you promise me this?' And the wolf, bowing his head, gave a clear sign that he did so promise. And Saint Francis said: 'Brother Wolf, I want you to give me a pledge that you will keep this promise so that I can trust you.' And when Saint Francis held out his hand to receive the pledge, the wolf lifted up his right front paw and gently placed it in the hand of Saint Francis, thus providing him with whatever sign he could of his pledge.

Then Saint Francis said: 'Brother Wolf, I command you in the name of Jesus Christ to come with me now without any distrust, and we will go and confirm this peace in the name of God.' And the wolf went with him obediently, just like a pet lamb. When the townspeople saw this they were utterly amazed, and at once the news spread through the whole region, and all the people—great and small, men and women, young and old—flocked to the market-place to see the wolf with Saint Francis.

[Saint Francis then preached them a sermon, telling them that if they were so afraid of the jaws of an ordinary wolf, how much more should they fear the jaws of Hell. 'Turn to God, therefore, my beloved, and do fitting penance for your sins; and God will deliver you from the wolf in this world and from eternal fire in the world to come.' The wolf and the people then promise to keep their respective parts of the bargain— the wolf will not harm them, and they will feed the wolf—and the wolf again gave his pledge to Saint Francis by giving him his paw.]

The said wolf then lived in Gubbio for two years and used to go from door to door, tamely entering the houses, doing harm to no-one and being harmed by none. The people were kind to him and fed him, and as he went around the town and through the houses, not a single dog ever barked at him. At last, after two years, Brother Wolf died of old age, and the townspeople were deeply grieved; for when they saw him going tamely around the town, they were better reminded of the virtues and holiness of Saint Francis. To the praise of Christ. Amen.

Francis and the Turtle-Doves

One day, a young lad had snared a number of turtle-doves and was taking them to sell when Saint Francis met him. The saint, who had a particular compassion for gentle animals, looked at the doves with a tender glance and said to the youngster: 'Good lad, I beg you, give me those doves so that such gentle and innocent birds, which, in the Holy Scriptures, are likened to pure, humble, and faithful souls, do not fall into the hands of cruel people who will kill them.'

Inspired by God, the youngster immediately gave all of them to Saint Francis; and he, taking them to his bosom, began to speak sweetly to them: 'My little sisters, you simple doves, innocent and pure, why do you let yourselves be caught? It is now my wish to save you from death and make nests for you, so that you may be fruitful and multiply, according to the command of God your Creator.'

Then Saint Francis went and made nests for them all, and they, making use of them, began to lay eggs and rear their young in the very sight of the friars. They stayed there so tamely and became so used to Saint Francis and the other friars that they seemed like chickens that had been raised by them from birth. Nor did they leave until Saint Francis, with his blessing, gave them permission to go.

And Saint Francis said to the youngster who had given them to him: 'My son, one day you will be a friar in this Order and graciously serve Jesus Christ.' And so it turned out: for the said youngster did become a friar and lived in the Order in great holiness. To the praise of Christ. Amen.

GODRIC OF FINCHALE

The Greedy Deer

[After he had settled at Finchale and built his little oratory, Godric gave himself up to a life of prayer, meditation, contemplation, penance, and severe asceticism (his austerities certainly equalled—and sometimes surpassed—those of the Desert Fathers). But he knew, as his biographer tells us, that to spend too long on one thing can lead to boredom and a loss of spirit and he would therefore turn his hands to various activities whilst keeping his mind still fixed on God. One of these activities, and what happened as a result of it, is described in the following anecdote:]

In his immediate neighbourhood he had uprooted the unfruitful undergrowth in the wood and had begun to graft cuttings of fruit trees onto the tree trunks that were left. These cuttings, to which he attended with such skill, he had collected from various visitors, and from them he made for himself a sort of enclosed garden. In the summer, when the tender shoots began to live again and bring forth their green leaves, the cuttings he had grafted onto the tree trunks also began to grow, and tentatively, here and there, delicate foliage and tender leaves blossomed forth. But the limitless sweetness of their taste also attracted the wild animals of the wood, and they began to eat this unusual greenery with the greatest avidity and would very often meet at this pasture for their food. They would tear off the leaves of the apple trees as well as the apples, and would destroy the tender saplings either by chewing off their bark or by scattering them with their hooves. There was not one single kind of tree which the man  of God had planted with so much labour that these wild creatures of the woods, with their unbridled appetites, allowed to come to maturity.

So one day, when the man of God came out of his oratory, he saw a wild woodland stag pulling off the tender foliage of his trees and doing its best to scatter and spoil it. He went up to the creature, commanding it just by crooking his finger not to stir from the spot, but to wait there motionless till he arrived. O what a wondrous mystery! How strange and stupendous! This stag, this wild creature of the wood, which knew nothing of discretion, understood the will and command of the man of God from his gesture alone! Standing there, it was trembling all over, for it was aware, perhaps, that it had offended against the soul of the man of God. But he was so moved by its trembling and terror that he checked both his anger and the blows he had intended to give the animal; and as he approached, it humbled itself on its knees as if to ask forgiveness in whatever way it could for its rash transgression. The saint came up to it, took off the belt he had round his waist, put it round the neck of the kneeling creature, and in this way led it beyond the boundaries of his garden and the fence which surrounded it, let it go and told it to go free wherever it wanted.

Not long after this, however, a whole herd of the woodland creatures came there in a crowd. They leaped across the fence which enclosed the plot, ripped off the tender leaves and fragile flowers, and then busied themselves with tearing to pieces or breaking down or trampling underfoot every last one of the slips of the apple trees which he had first attended to in his garden, planting them and grafting them. Then out came the man of God and ordered the whole crowd not to leave the place. He seized a stick, hit one of them three times on her flank, and led her to the tree trunks which were the only things left. There he showed her by signs rather than words the harm her herd had done to the slips he had transplanted. Then he raised both his hands and his voice and said: 'In the name of Jesus of Nazareth, be off and away with you as fast as you can! And until these trees come to their full growth, do not dare to come and damage my garden again! The slips of the fruit trees that I have grafted onto these trunks are intended to feed people, not animals!' And with these words he threatened the rest of the dumb animals with the stick he held in his hand. The whole herd then went out, their heads bowed, stepping in an orderly fashion; and whereas they had earlier run wild, jumping hither and thither, and bounding about with the longest kind of leaps, they now went out step by step, their hooves twinkling along in decorous paces. He drove the whole herd right into the depths of the woods; but if any succumbed to weariness, he gently put his arms around them and led them out of his enclosure by raising the barrier for them. From that time on, no beast of the forest touched the young trees he had grafted, and not one of them presumed to transgress the boundaries which he had established for them.

Godric's Care of the Animals

The kindness of his devout heart was not only manifested in his helping human beings, but in his wise care he even looked after the reptiles and animals of the earth. For when all around was frozen hard in the cold of winter, he would go about barefoot, and if he found any animal help-less or dying in the bitter cold, he would tuck it into his armpit or hold it against his chest until it warmed up again. The devout searcher would very often go around the thick hedges and dense patches of brambles, and if by chance he came across an animal that had lost its way or was cowed by the harsh weather or was exhausted or dying, he would heal it with whatever medical skills he possessed. And if anyone in his service had caught a bird or little creature in a trap or snare or noose, he would snatch it out of their hands as soon as he learned of it and let it go free in the fields or woodland glades. Many times, therefore, the trappers would hide the prey they had captured under a corn-measure or basket or in some place even more secret than these, but they were never able to fool him or keep it hidden. For often, without being told—or indeed, with his servant stoutly denying it—he would go quickly to the place where they had hidden the creatures, and with his servants covered in a confusion of shame and fear, he would lift them out and release them. In the same way, he would take into his house hares and other beasts who were fleeing from the hunters, and when the huntsmen had

gone home, their hopes frustrated, he would send them away
to those places in the woods with which they were familiar.
Many and many a time the dumb animals of the woodlands
would swerve aside from the hunters' traps and flee to his
hut for protection, for it might have been that by some divine
inspiration they were certain that they would there be provided
with a safe refuge.

The Obedient Cow

[Although we know that Godric had made a garden
for himself, and although he realised that manual labour could
be both useful and fulfilling, his prime concern was, of course,
his devotion to God and to the Mother of God. Accordingly,
since he spent so much time in prayer and meditation, it was
necessary for him to have someone around the place to look after his frugal needs and attend to the various daily tasks which
needed to be done. At first, therefore, a little lad came to serve
him—he was the son of his brother—and stayed with him for
eleven years, but at the time the following tale took place, the
youngster was still very much a child, and, like many of us,
did not like getting up early in the morning:]
      At that time the man of God possessed nothing living
save a single cow, but because the lad was still small and very
young, he would often be so sleepy in the mornings that he
would forget to take the animal out to pasture or bring her
back again in the evening, or perhaps the work had become
boring to him because of its repetitiveness. So one day the man
of God went up to the beast, put his belt around her neck,
and spoke to her as if she had reason and intelligence: 'Come
and follow me,' he said, 'and walk with me to your pasture.'
Off she went with him, but the young lad, who had seen and
heard all this, followed them. Then the man of God spoke
again to the cow: 'I command you in the name of the Lord

that every day at sunrise, without anyone leading you, you go forth on your own to your pasture; and every noon and evening, when the proper time comes, you come home without any servant to guide you. And when your udders are full of milk and need milking, come to me wherever I am, and then, when you have been milked and if there is still time, go back relieved to your pasture.' And wonderful and astonishing though it may be, from that day forth the cow always went out and came back at the correct time, and whenever in the day her udders were filled with rich milk, she would come to him. And if he happened to be in church, she would stand outside the door, lowing and mooing, as if asking for him. Then, when he had finished his hour of prayer, he would come out and milk her, and she would then go away to her proper place.

Sometime later, however, another youngster had taken the place of the first one in the house of the man of God, and it was to him that these outside tasks were allotted. He did not know, however, how the cow was used to obeying the instructions of the  man of God, and one day, when he found her grazing in the fields, he began to harass her and move her on by prodding her with a stick. She was naturally offended at this and charged at the lad as fast as she could: she caught him up on her horns, and in rage and fury carried him to the door of the house where the man of God was staying. He came out and put his arms around the youngster, lifted him off the horns, and rescued him unhurt from the anger of the offended animal.

This very youngster, who is now an old, old man, would often tell this tale with thankfulness, praising the Lord who, by the merits of his master, had so wonderfully deigned to snatch him from sudden death.

God Knows!

In the time of Ranulf, bishop of Durham, some of his household had come out to go hunting, and they and their hounds were pursuing a stag which they had singled out as being more beautiful than the others. Their quarry, driven on by the clamour and the barking, fled to Godric's hermitage, and bleating piteously, seemed to demand his aid. When the venerable man came out and saw the beast standing at his

gate, exhausted and trembling, he was moved with pity; so he commanded it to cease its bleating, opened the door of his little hut, and let it go in. The stag at once humbled itself at the father's feet, but he, sensing that the hunters were drawing nearer, went outside again, closed the door behind him, and sat down in the open.

Now in the meantime, the hounds had returned to their masters, barking furiously as if aggrieved by the loss of their prey; but the hunters still continued to follow the tracks of the stag. They circled around the area, forcing their way through the almost impenetrable thickets of thorns and brambles and cutting a path with their weapons: and then they came upon the man of God wearing his worthless rags. But when they asked him about the stag, he had no intention of betraying his guest and replied prudently: 'God knows where he might be!' And they, looking at the angelic beauty of his face and revering his holiness and sanctity, fell prostrate before him and asked his pardon for their rash intrusion. Often afterwards they would tell of the wondrous thing which had happened to them there, and by repeating it frequently they handed it down to the memory of those that came after them. The stag, however, stayed with Godric until the evening, and he then let it go free. But for many years after it would turn aside from its path and come to lie at his feet, so that in this way it could show its thanks for its deliverance.

HELLE

Helle and the Wild Asses

On one occasion Helle went to visit his own brothers, and when he had admonished them well, he hastened back into the desert carrying with him some supplies suited to his needs. Seeing some wild she-asses grazing, he said to them: 'In the name of Christ, let one of you come here and take my burden.' One of them immediately hurried over to him, and after he had settled his baggage on her, he mounted her himself and reached his cave in a single day. After he had spread out the loaves and fruit in the sun, the wild animals came up  to them when, as usual, they were going to the spring; but if they touched so much as a single loaf, they expired.

Helle's Taxi

One Sunday, he went to see some monks and said to
them: 'Why have you not attended to your worship today?'
They told him that it was because the priest had not come from
across the river. 'I shall go and call him', he said to them. But
they told him that it was impossible for anyone to cross at
the ford, not only because of the depth of the water, but also
because there was a huge beast at that spot, a crocodile which
had devoured many people.

Helle, however, did not hesitate. He got up at once and
hurried to the ford, and the beast immediately took him on its
back and set him down on the other bank. He then found the
priest in his place and implored him not to neglect the community of brothers. When the priest saw the patched rag that
he was wearing, he was amazed at his humility and frugality,
and said: 'You have a most beautiful garment for your soul,
brother!' He then followed Helle back to the river. But because
they could not find a ferry, abba Helle gave a shout to summon the crocodile. It obeyed him immediately and flattened its
back for them to ride on. Helle asked the priest to get on with
him, but when he saw the beast he was terrified and backed
away; and as he and the brothers who lived over the river
looked on in horror, Helle and the beast crossed the ford. But
when he came to the other side, he dragged the beast onto
the bank with him and said: 'It is better for you to die and
pay the price for all the lives you have taken.' And the beast
immediately lay down and expired.

ILLTUD

Illtud, Samson, and the Thieving Birds

When the harvest was ripening in autumn, birds began to eat the harvest of Saint Illtud and leave the ears virtually empty. When he found out about this, Saint Illtud grieved for his loss and ordered his pupils to take turns in guarding the crop each day, continually slinging stones the whole time.

When it was the turn of the disciple Samson, he was ready and more than willing to fulfil his master's command, but although he kept guard as best he could, he could not keep the corn safe and untouched.

So, because he knows no other possible way of defending the crop since there were so many criminals, he seeks divine counsel and help as to how he can confine the multitudinous birds. Inspired by divine counsel, he consulted with himself and, on reflection, discovered what he should do. To him was given the divine power to drive away the birds from the crop by rendering them incapable of flight. They try to fly, but all their efforts are in vain. When the kind-hearted Samson saw this, he made them march in front of him of their own free-will, just like tame animals. Driven in this way, they come to the open door of the barn and go inside: like horses or sheep, those in front lead those  behind, and like sheep or horses, the further they walk, the tamer they become. With no net to hold them in, the birds stay completely confined. They have been tamed by the divine power which keeps the stars in check. Mournfully they sing, hungry and fasting; from their well-deserved prison they pour forth mournful songs. There was lamentation among the company for the freedom they were seeking; they were repentant for having wasted so many ears of grain. But in his compassion, Saint Illtud frees the imprisoned flocks; and after this miracle they injured him never again.

JEROME

The Lion and the Donkey

One day, as evening was drawing nigh, the blessed Jerome was sitting with his brothers, as is the custom of monks, to hear a reading from the holy Scripture and to make clear the divine precepts. Suddenly there came into the monastery cloister a great lion: it was limping on three legs and holding the fourth off the ground. When they saw it, many of the brothers fled in terror (so fearful is human frailty), but Saint Jerome went to meet it as if it were a guest. The lion, of course, could not speak, for that was not its nature, so when they met it did what it could and held out to the said father its paw, which had an injury in the pad. Then the saint called the brothers and ordered them to wash the wounded paw carefully and so discover why the lion was limping. When they made a close examination, they found that the lion's pad had been pierced by thorns. They therefore carefully applied the necessary remedies to cure the wound and it quickly healed.

The lion now put aside all its animal savagery and wildness, and began to go here and there among them just like a quiet, domestic animal. When he learned of this, the blessed Jerome spoke to the brothers like this: 'My brothers, I ask each of you to consider this question with the greatest care: what work can we find for this lion to do? We need something suitable for him yet useful for us: something he can do easily and perform efficiently. For I firmly believe that God sent him here not so much to cure his foot (for he could have healed that without us), but rather to make it clear to us by this visit that he is wonderfully eager to provide us with whatever assistance our needs may require.'

Then the said brothers, humbly and of one accord, gave their father this reply: 'You are well aware, father, that the donkey who brings us the wood we use from the forest needs someone to look after him, for we are always afraid that he will be eaten by some cruel beast. So if it pleases you and if it seems right to you, let this lion take charge of our donkey: he can lead him out to the pasture and then bring him home again.' And so it was done. The donkey was put in the charge of the lion who acted as his shepherd: they always took the road to the pasture  together, and wherever the donkey grazed, there was his defender—the surest of all defenders! But in order for the lion to eat and the donkey to complete his appointed task, he would always come home with him at the usual hours.

This went on for a considerable time, but one day, after he had taken the donkey to the pasture, the lion was overcome with immeasurable drowsiness and fell fast asleep. But while the lion was sunk in deep slumber some merchants happened to come walking along the road on their way to buy oil in Egypt. They saw the donkey grazing, and when they noticed that there was no-one there to guard him, they were consumed by wicked greed and seized the donkey and took him with them.

When the lion woke up, he knew nothing of the loss that had occurred, and went to look for the grazing animal which had been put in his care. But when he was not to be seen in the place where he usually grazed, the lion was overwhelmed with concern, anxiety, and grief; and for the rest of the day he went roaring hither and thither looking for what he had lost. But when at last all hope of finding the donkey had gone, he came and stood at the gate of the monastery. He was well aware of his guilt, and did not dare go in as he used to do when he had the donkey with him.

When blessed Jerome and the brothers saw him waiting at the monastery gate without the donkey, and because he had failed to return at his usual hour, they concluded that he had been driven by hunger to kill his animal. They therefore had no intention of giving him his usual meal and said: 'Away with you! Eat whatever you've left of the donkey and fill your greedy belly with that!' But even as they said this, they were uncertain as to whether he had actually done this wicked deed.

The brothers therefore went to the pasture where the lion used to take the animal, and they hunted far and wide to see if they could find some clue as to its death. But when they found no trace of the slaughter, they hurried back to tell all this to the blessed Jerome. When he heard it, he said to the brothers: 'I implore you, brothers, even though you've sustained the loss of a donkey, don't let this provoke you and don't abandon the lion. Treat him as you did before: give him his food and feed him—but let him take the place of the donkey. Make a light harness for him so that he can go into the woods and drag back our wood for us.' And so it was done.

While the lion was regularly attending to this servile labour, the time came for the merchants to return. And one day, when he had finished his work, he made his way to the field—and even though he was a dumb animal, I think that this was the consequence of divine prompting. He ran in circles, now here, now there, wanting to know more about what had happened to his companion. Finally, utterly exhausted but

still concerned, he climbed to a piece of high ground near the
public highway so that he could look around. Far away he
spied some men coming towards him. They had laden camels,
and in front of them walked a donkey. As yet they were still
too far away for him to recognise the animal, but for all that he
set off, very cautiously, to meet them.

Now it is said to be the custom in that country that
whenever people set off on a long journey with their camels,
a donkey with a camel's halter on its neck always leads the
way, and the camels follow behind it. So when the travellers—
the merchants, that is—came nearer to the lion, he recognised
the donkey. Roaring savagely, he burst forth upon them; but
although he made an immense noise, he injured none of them.
They were mad with terror (as well they might be!) and immediately turned to flee, leaving everything behind. When
they had fled, the lion lashed the ground with his tail, roaring
terribly all the while, and began to drive the terrified camels,
laden as they were, before him to the monastery.

When the brothers saw this unusual spectacle—the
donkey leading the way, the camels with their burdens in the
middle, and the lion bringing up the rear—they slipped away
quickly and quietly to tell the blessed Jerome. When he heard,
he came out and kindly commanded them to open the monastery gates. He also ordered them to keep total silence, and
said: 'Remove the loads from these guests of ours—the donkey
and the camels, I mean—and bathe their feet and give them
fodder, and wait to see what God wants to show his servants
by means of this event.'

Then, when everything had been done for the camels
as he had ordered, the lion began to go joyfully here and there
through the cloister just as he did of old, flattening himself at
the feet of the various brothers and wagging his tail, as if asking forgiveness for a crime he had never committed. When the
brothers saw this, they were truly penitent for having brought
against him a charge of such cruelty: 'Behold our shepherd!',
they were saying. 'A short time ago we cruelly condemned

him for having devoured our donkey, but the Lord has
deigned to send him back to us with this praiseworthy miracle

in order to have the
charge removed!'
But the blessed
Jerome, who knew
what was going to
happen next, spoke
to the brothers like
this: 'My brothers,
there are guests on
their way to us:
prepare everything
necessary for
refreshment so that they may be received, as they should be,
without embarrassment.' And no sooner had he given the orders, than they were swiftly fulfilled.

Having done as he commanded, the brothers were
talking with the blessed Jerome, when there suddenly came
a messenger who said that there were guests at the gate of
the monastery who wanted to see the father of the community. This father, of whom we have now so often heard, ordered them to open the gates and let them come in to him.
But despite this invitation, they entered shamefaced, and when
they saw the blessed Jerome, they prostrated themselves at his
feet and implored forgiveness for their fault. He kindly raised
them up and admonished them to use their own property with
thankfulness, but not to seize or meddle with that of others: in
short, always to live prudently in the presence of God. When
he had finished this excellent discourse, he bade them accept
refreshment, take back their camels, and go their way. Then
all of them cried out with one voice: 'Father, we implore you:
deign to accept half the oil which the camels brought for the
lamps in the church and the needs of the brothers; for we
know for a certainty that it was more for your advantage than
for ours that we went to Egypt to do business.' But the blessed

Jerome said: 'What you ask certainly isn't right! It would indeed seem harsh if we, who ought to have compassion on others and relieve their needs by our gifts, should bear down on you by taking what is yours when we have no need of it.' Then they said: 'We will touch neither this food nor anything that is ours unless you first command that what we request be done. So as we have said, accept now half the oil that the camels brought—and from now on we and our heirs promise to deliver to you and your successors a gallon and a half of oil every year.' And so, constrained and compelled by their urgent entreaties, the blessed Jerome commanded that what they asked be fulfilled. They then took their meal, received both his blessing and their camels, and returned joyfully and gladly to their own people.

JESUS OF NAZARETH

The Procession of the Animals

[Having been warned in a dream of the impending Massacre of the Innocents, Joseph and Mary took the infant Jesus and fled away to Egypt; and it is on the first and second days of their journey that the following events took place:]

When they arrived at a certain cave and wanted to rest there, Mary got down from her donkey and sat there with Jesus in her lap. With Joseph there were three boys and with Mary a girl, all of whom were making the journey. Suddenly there came out of the cave a number of dragons, and when they saw them the boys cried out in great fear. Then Jesus got down from his mother's lap and stood on his feet in front of the dragons: they worshipped him, and after worshipping him, they went away. Then was fulfilled that which was spoken by the prophet David: 'Praise the Lord from the earth, you dragons, you dragons and all deeps' (Ps 148:7). The little child Jesus, walking in front of them, commanded them to hurt no one; but Mary and Joseph were very much afraid that the little child might perhaps be hurt by the dragons. Jesus said to them: 'Do not be afraid; and do not think that I am a little child. I was and am always a perfect man, and it is necessary that all the wild beasts of the forests shall become tame before me.'

Similarly, lions and leopards worshipped him and accompanied them in the desert. Wherever Mary and Joseph went, they preceded them, showing them the way; and bowing their heads, they worshipped Jesus. The first day that Mary saw the lions and the various kinds of wild animals coming round them, she was utterly terrified. But the child Jesus, smiling, looked her in the face and said: 'Don't be afraid, mother; they are hurrying here to serve you, not to harm you.' And with these words he drove out the fear from their hearts.

The lions walked with them and with the oxen and asses and other beasts which were carrying what they needed; and although they all stayed together, the lions never harmed them, but were tame among the sheep and rams which they had with them and which they had brought with them from Judaea. They walked among wolves and were never afraid, and not one was hurt by another. Then was fulfilled that which was spoken by the prophet: 'Wolves shall feed with lambs; the lion and the ox shall eat straw together' (Is 65:25). With them were two oxen and a cart to carry what they needed, and these the lions guarded on their journey.

The Superiority of the Animals

There is a road which leaves Jericho and leads to the River Jordan, to the place where the children of Israel crossed and where the Ark of the Covenant is said to have rested. Jesus, who was then eight years old, left Jericho and went to the Jordan. On the way there was a cave near the Jordan where a lioness was rearing her cubs, and no-one could go along the road in safety. But when Jesus was on his way from Jericho, he knew that the lioness had given birth to her young in that cave, and he entered it in the sight of all. But when the lions saw Jesus, they ran to meet him and worshipped him. And Jesus sat in the cavern with the lion cubs scampering around his feet, rubbing up against him and playing. The older lions stood at a distance, their heads bowed, and worshipped him, and wagged their tails in front of him.

Then the people who were standing a long way away and who could not see Jesus said: 'Unless either he or his parents had committed some grievous sins, he would not have given himself up to the lions willingly.' And when the people were pondering this among themselves and were standing around in great sorrow, suddenly, in the sight of the people, Jesus came out of the cave, and before his feet were the lions, playing among themselves. The parents of Jesus, with bowed heads, stood far away and watched, and so too the people stood far away, since they dared not approach the lions. Then Jesus began to speak to the people: 'How much better than you are the animals who know their Lord and glorify him; but you people, made in the image and likeness of God, are ignorant!

The animals know me and become tame; but people see me
and do not know me!'

After this, in the sight of all, Jesus crossed the Jordan
with the lions, and the water of the Jordan was divided to
the right hand and the left. Then he said this to the lions so
that everyone could hear: 'Go in peace and harm no one; nor
will anyone harm you until you return whence you set out.'
And so they bade him farewell, not with their voices but with
bodily gestures, and went away to their own places. Jesus then
returned to his mother.

JOHN THE EVANGELIST

What the Animals Do at Night

[After his resurrection, Christ has come back to the
Mount of Olives and has gathered to him all his disciples. John,
the beloved disciple, then takes advantage of his position, re-
minds Christ that he was his favourite, and asks him if he
might be permitted a guided tour of heaven and its mysteries.
Christ willingly agrees to this, summons one of the cherubim
to act as a guide, and dispatches Saint John to the heavenly
realms. After seeing a multitude of wonders and experiencing
the most marvellous revelations, John becomes interested in the
way in which the twenty-four hours of the day are arranged
and proportioned. He questions the cherub on the matter and
the following conversation takes place:]

I said to him: 'My lord, how are the limits set on the
hours of the night and day?'

He said to me: 'Listen and I will tell you. God has
placed twelve cherubim outside the veil. They do no work
at all, but chant twelve hymns every day. When the first has
ended his hymn, the first hour has ended; when the second has

ended his hymn, the second hour has ended; and so on down to the twelfth. When the twelfth cherub has ended, the twelfth hour has ended.'

I said to him: 'With regard to the twelve hours of the night: are there seraphim appointed over them or not?'

He said to me: 'No. But when the animals, the birds, and the reptiles offer up their prayer, the first hour has ended; when the second hour has ended, the beasts again raise their voices; and so down to the twelfth hour of the night. It is the living creatures of God which set limits upon them.'

JOHN I

A Horse Knows Its Place

In the time of the Goths, the most blessed man John, pontiff of the church of Rome, was on his way to see Justin, the eastern emperor. When he arrived at Corinth he found himself in need of a saddle-horse so that he could continue his journey. A certain nobleman there heard of this and offered him the horse which, because of its great gentleness, his wife was accustomed to ride—but when John came to some other place where a suitable horse could be found, then for the sake of the nobleman's wife, he was to send back the one he had been given.

And so it happened that as soon as the pope had been escorted on the horse as far as a certain place and had found another, he sent back the one he had borrowed. But when the wife of the said nobleman wanted to mount the horse, as was her custom, she could no longer do so, for after carrying such a pontiff, it refused to carry the woman. With great snorts and snufflings, and with continual balkings of its whole body, it seemed to indicate its disdain, for after bearing the limbs of the pope, it could not possibly carry a woman. The nobleman wisely suspected this, and immediately sent the horse back to the venerable man, imploring and entreating him to keep the horse for himself, for by his riding it, it had been dedicated to his service.

JUDAH THE PRINCE

Karma

[Rabbi Judah the Prince (we are told in the Talmud) said: 'Suffering is precious', but the sufferings of Rabbi Eleazar ben Rabbi Simeon were superior in the virtue they accrued to those of Rabbi Judah. Why? Because those of Rabbi Eleazar ben Rabbi Simeon came to him through love and left him through love, but those of Rabbi Judah came to him because of a particular incident, and left him because of a particular incident.]

'They came to him because of a particular incident.' What was it? On one occasion Rabbi Judah the Prince was sitting delivering a religious discourse to an assembly of Babylonian Jews in Sepphoris and a calf which was being led to slaughter broke loose. It went to the rabbi, placed its head in his lap, and lowed, as if to say: 'Save me!' But Rabbi Judah said: 'What can I do? Go! It was for this purpose that you were created.' They therefore said in heaven: 'Since he has no mercy,

let us bring sufferings upon him.' And so it happened that
Rabbi Judah suffered from toothache for thirteen years.

'And left him because of a particular incident.' What
was it? One day, when the rabbi's maidservant was sweeping
the house, she came across some young weasels and was about
to kill them. 'Let them be', said the rabbi, 'for it is written:

"And his mercies are over all his works" (Ps 145:9)'. They
therefore said in heaven: 'Since he has shown mercy, let us
show mercy to him'. And his toothache ceased immediately.

KEVIN

Saint Kevin at Prayer

[After founding Glendalough and ensuring that its
administration and religious life were in good hands, Kevin
himself retired to a tiny hut about a mile from the monastery
and forbade his monks to bring him any food or to come near
the place unless there was a very good reason. 'And the wild
creatures of the mountains and the woods, made tame, would
keep Saint Kevin company, and, like domestic creatures, would
drink water from his hands.' After seven years of this idyllic
existence, the saint moved to the northern shore of the Upper
Lake at Glendalough where he built himself a little oratory,

and it was there that he was living in complete isolation when the following events took place:]

One day the huntsman of the king of Leinster was following his hounds who were following a boar, and he came into the valley. The boar went into the little oratory of Saint Kevin, but the hounds would not enter and lay down on their bellies outside the door. And there, under a tree, Saint Kevin was praying: many birds were perched on his hands and his shoulders or flying round about him, singing sweet songs to the saint of God.

When the huntsman saw these things, he was astounded, and letting the boar go free because of the blessing of the holy hermit, he immediately returned home with his hounds. He then told the king and all the others about the miracle he had witnessed.

Saint Kevin and the Blackbird

One Lent, Saint Kevin had as usual fled from human company to a certain solitary spot. Here, in a little hut which merely kept out the sun and rain, he abandoned himself to contemplation, spending his time in reading and prayer. While he was praying in his usual fashion, his hand stretched out of the window and raised to heaven, it happened that a blackbird settled upon it, treated it as if it were her own nest, and laid her eggs in it. But so great was the patience of the saint and so moved was he with compassion that he neither closed his hand nor drew it in, but held it out untiringly in the required shape until the chicks were fully hatched. In perpetual memory of this remarkable occurrence, all the images of Saint Kevin throughout Ireland have a blackbird in his outstretched hand.

The Greedy Ravens

[Some years later, Colman, one of the Leinster chieftains, married a woman of high rank, but finding that they were incompatible, he separated from her and married another. The rejected wife was incensed at this and, being adept at magic and witchcraft, brought about the death of all the children born to her successor. In his old age, however, Colman had a son, Faoláin, and in order to save him from the wiles and devices of his former wife, he asked Saint Kevin if he would accept the child, bring him up, and offer him the protection of his undoubted sanctity:]

Saint Kevin gladly received him and brought him up as a layman, just as his father had instructed, and he loved him dearly. But because women and cows were far from his monastery, Saint Kevin did not know where to get fresh milk to feed the little baby. He therefore prayed to God to give him some help, and God immediately sent Saint Kevin a doe from the nearby mountain, and on her milk the baby Faoláin was reared. Until the child grew up, the doe would come twice a day to Saint Kevin's monastery, and would there be milked by one of the brothers for the baby Faoláin. Then, wholly tame, she would return to her pasture.

One day, however, when the brother was milking her outside, he put down the pail of milk on the ground. Up came

a greedy raven intending to drink it, and with his beak knocked over the pail of milk onto the ground. Seeing this, Saint Kevin said to the raven: 'For a long time shall you and your race do penance for this crime: on the day of my departure to heaven a great deal of meat will be prepared, but you will not eat of it. And if any of you has the nerve to touch even the offal or the blood of the slaughtered beasts on those days, he shall die there and then. Everyone there will be merry; but you, on the peaks of these mountains around us, will be sad, cawing and quarrelling among your-selves in your sorrow.' And as the saint predicted, this miracle has been fulfilled every year until this very day.

LIBERTINUS

All For One and One For All

Libertinus was a most venerable man who had lived as a disciple of Honoratus and had been trained by him. In the time of Totila, king of the Goths, he was the prior of the monastery of Fondi. One day, when he was travelling on some monastic business in the province of Samnium, Darida, a Goth-ic general, arrived at the same place with his troops. His men threw the servant of God off the horse he was riding and stole it. He, however, took the loss of his mount quite cheerfully, and even offered the thieves the whip he was holding. 'Take this', he said, 'so that you have something with which to drive the horse.' And when he had said this to them, he immediately devoted himself to prayer.

The troops of the said general then rode off at a rapid pace, but when they came to the River Volturno, the horses stopped. The riders started to beat them with their spears and goad them with their spurs, but although they were able to torment the horses, flogging them with their whips and goring them with their spurs, they were unable to make them move. It was as if the water of the river were a fatal precipice, and they were terrified to approach it.

Then, when the horsemen had beaten them for a long time and worn themselves out, one of them suggested that  they were suffering this setback to their journey because of the wrong they had done to the servant of God when they were on their way there. They turned back at once, and after some time they found Libertinus still prostrate in prayer. But when they said to him: 'Get up and take your horse', he replied: 'Go in peace. I have no need of a horse.' But they dismounted, set him against his will on the horse from which they had pulled him, and immediately rode away. And when their horses arrived with all speed at the river they had earlier been unable to cross, they crossed it as if there were no water in the river-bed at all. So it was that after the one horse had been returned to the servant of God, all the soldiers regained control of their own mounts.

MACARIUS THE GREAT

The Price of a Mosquito

Early one day, Macarius was sitting in his cell when a mosquito landed on his foot and stung him. Feeling the pain, he killed it with his hand when it was gorged with blood. But he then accused himself of being vengeful and condemned himself to go into the inner desert and sit naked in the marsh of Scetis for six months. The mosquitoes there are like wasps and can pierce even the hides of wild boars. Macarius was soon bitten all over and he became so swollen that people thought he had elephantiasis. When he came back to his cell after six months, they knew that he was Macarius only by his voice.

Gratitude

On one occasion, they say, Macarius was praying in his cave in the desert. Nearby there happened to be another cave which was the den of a hyena, and while Macarius was praying the hyena came in and licked his feet. Then she gently took the hem of his garment and tugged him towards the cave where she lived. He followed her, saying: 'What does this animal want me to do?'

After she had led him to her cave, she went in and brought out to him her own cubs, which had been born blind. He put some spit on their eyes and prayed over them, and when he gave the cubs back to the hyena they could see. The mother suckled them, and then picked them up and went away. Next day, as an offering of thanks, she brought the huge skin of a great ram to the man and laid it at his feet. He smiled at her as if she possessed both reason and sensibility, took the skin, and spread it out under him. This skin is still pointed out today.

MAEDOC OF FERNS

The Invisible Stag

One day, when Saint Maedoc was staying in a secret place and reading there, an exhausted stag came to him, followed by hounds. The stag stood in front of the saint of God as

if asking for protection; and the man of God, knowing why it did so, placed his wax writing-tablet on its antlers. When the hounds came after it, the stag seemed to them to be a phantom. So since the hounds could neither find the stag there nor follow its tracks further, they went home. And the stag, putting down the man of God's writing-tablet from its antlers, escaped free.

MOLING

Share and Share Alike

The most blessed father Moling was very generous and kind to all: not only to people but also to animals, as the following story shows. One day, thirty hunting dogs came to him, worn out from their wanderings, and moved by compassion the saint arranged a place for them to rest and have their meal. The holy high-priest ordered thirty buttered loaves to be shared among them so that they would have enough to eat. But when the servants had prepared this, fifteen of the dogs went outside and were circling the monastery so that when they left they would know which way to go. When the servants were ready to take the food to the dogs, they told the holy father that fifteen of them were missing. The saint said to them: 'Give the whole of what you have prepared to those that are still here, and they will do whatever God's will reveals to them: they may eat everything or they may leave a share for their fellows. Let us go: the other dogs will soon be back.'

When the thirty loaves, loaded with butter, were put in front of the fifteen dogs, each of them took and ate a single loaf, and they neither touched nor ate any of the other fifteen loaves. When the other dogs also came in, they, likewise, each took and ate a single loaf. With their strength restored after their meal, they went outside to where the man of God was and with their ears and tails showed their happiness, as if thanking him for the food. The saint then gave them leave to depart and off they went, leaping and running on their way.

The Cat, the Wren, and the Fly

One day, when the holy priest Moling was sitting reading in a certain place with his servant, there came to him that bird which is called 'the druid of birds', since to some it provides omens; it is also the smallest of birds. In its beak it held a fly, alive and buzzing. But while the little bird was eating the fly in front of the man of God, a cat seized the bird itself, killed it on the spot, and began to eat it greedily. When Saint Moling saw this misfortune, he was moved by compassion and commanded the cat to give back the little bird from her jaws. And straightaway, as soon as she heard the saint's command, the cat, fearful and trembling, spat out the bird from her throat onto the ground. It was dead and half-eaten. The holy priest made the sign of the cross over the bird's corpse and it rose up alive and well, still stained with its own blood. The saint then commanded it to disgorge before him the fly which it had swallowed, and the little bird immediately disgorged the fly from its stomach like a tiny piece of dung. The holy man blessed this monstrous little lump, and there-

upon the fly got up, healthy as ever, and flew around buzzing. The bird flew back to her own kind, chirping happily.

Seeing this, the servant of Saint Moling went out to the brothers and told them of these wonders, saying in parables: 'Brothers, I have just seen the resurrection of the dead from their narrow graves!' And the brothers, knowing that this was true, gave glory to Christ.

Saint Moling's Fox and the Hens

It was the custom of the most blessed high-priest Moling to feed animals, both wild and domestic, in honour of their Creator, and they used to take food from his hand. Among them was a fox. One day, this fox stole a hen which belonged to the brothers and ate it. When the brothers complained about this, the man of God scolded the fox and accused him of being more dishonest than all the other animals. Seeing that his master was angry with him, the fox went off to the cell of some nuns who were living under the care of Saint Moling, and once there, craftily seized a hen, brought it to the saint, and offered it to him alive and well. The saint smiled and said: 'For what you stole you offer what you have seized! Take this hen back to her mistresses and deliver her to them unharmed. And afterwards live without thieving, like the other animals.' When he heard this, the fox picked up the hen in his teeth and laid her down unharmed in the cell of her mistresses. And those who witnessed the working of such a miracle in both places rejoiced over it and praised God.

Bibliophagy

On another occasion, a different fox stole a book belonging to the brothers and hid it outside in one of his earths, intending to eat it at leisure later. But on returning to the monastery he was found carrying off a honeycomb and eating that. The brothers then seized him, brought him to Saint Moling, and accused him of stealing the book. The holy old man ordered the brothers to set him free and when he was released the saint said to him: 'You cunning and crafty creature! Go as fast as you can and bring that book  back to me undamaged.' At these words, the fox went out and brought back the book from his hole with all speed, dry and undamaged. He put it at the feet of the holy priest and then lay flat on the ground in front of the man of God as if asking for forgiveness. The saint said to him: 'Get up, you wretched creature; don't be afraid! But never again will you remove a book!' Then the fox joyfully got up and carried out the saint's instructions in a wonderful way: for after this not only did he not touch any books, but if anyone so much as showed him a book for a joke, he would flee away from him.

The Last Visit of the Foxes

When the most blessed priest Moling was in the city of Ferns, a host of foxes gathered in the woods and afterwards came straight to the city of Ferns. They passed through the city to the place where the holy priest Moling was, and, in a wonderful way, not a single dog nor any person harmed these foxes or hunted them either on their way to the holy old man Moling or when they were returning from him. When people saw them, they would say that they were going to the saint of God, Moling; whereas the dogs were held back by a divine command.

The holy old man Moling foretold their arrival to his disciples, saying prophetically: 'Some unusual guests will come to us soon who, up to now, have never dwelt with people; nor will they stay with them for long.' But until the foxes arrived, his disciples had no idea of what guests he was speaking. He ordered a lodging to be made ready for them, well strewn with straw, and when the foxes came, the man of God went out into the courtyard to meet them. When they saw him, the foxes, one by one, joyfully came to his feet and the holy priest received them with the greatest kindness. That night they stayed there and were thoroughly refreshed, and everyone was amazed at the respect which the foxes showed for the holy man.

Next day, when the foxes were ready to go back and the joy they had felt earlier had changed to sorrow, Saint Moling said to them: 'In a little while I shall leave this city and go back to my own place.' And at these words, the foxes became

even more sorrowful. The saint of God then blessed them and they returned to their own places.

But some astute men, who had heard the holy old man say to the foxes: 'In a little while I shall leave this city and go back to my own place,' guessed rightly and said that he was telling them that he had only a little while left in this world. And both people and animals alike were saddened at these words.

MOLUA

The Wolves' Banquet

One day, the holy father Molua went to inspect the cattle belonging to his monastery; and among the trees near

the road he saw some wolves who were hungry, howling at the sky. Moved by compassion he took them with him and lodged them in the guest-house: he bathed their feet, had a calf killed and cooked, and looked after them with every kindness. And Saint Molua made it a yearly custom to provide such a banquet for the wolves. Afterwards the contented wolves began to guard the cattle of Saint Molua from other wolves and from thieves. Together with the saint's shepherds, they were just like members of the household, each knowing the other; and the wolves did this for many days even after Saint Molua's death.

MOSHE LEIB OF SASOV

God's Work

It was the custom of Rabbi Moshe, the Sassover, to go to the annual fairs to see if there was anyone in need of his help. It happened once that for some reason the cattle-dealers had left their livestock unprovided for in the market-place and the heads of the calves were hanging with thirst. The Sassover ran up, took a pail in his hand, and watered the calves with as much skill as if it were his regular occupation. Just then one of  the dealers returned, and when he saw a man watering the calves, he asked him to attend to his own animals too, and promised to pay him for doing so. The rabbi obeyed; but when the man wanted to give him some money, he said: 'Get away, you fool! I take no payment for this. It says in the Psalm: "He is merciful to all his creatures" (Ps 145: 9); and what this saying implies is that just as He, God, is merciful, so should you, too, be merciful. So it is not your instructions I have obeyed, but the command of God.'

MOSES

Why Moses?

Our rabbis have taught that when our teacher Moses (peace be upon him!) was tending the flock of Jethro, his father-in-law, in the desert, a young kid escaped from him. He followed it until it reached a place where leek-plants were growing, and when the kid reached the plants it saw a pool of water and stopped to drink. When Moses came up to it, he said: 'I did not know that you ran away because you were thirsty: now you must be tired.' So he picked up the kid, put it on his shoulder, and walked back to his flock. The Holy One, blessed be He, said: 'Because you have shown mercy in leading the flock of a mortal man, you shall surely lead *my* flock, Israel.'

MUHAMMAD

Love of Cats Is Part of Faith

One day, some students seeking knowledge came from Jand and Khojand to ask our Master Jalāl-ud-Dīn Rūmī the following question: 'In this world of forms, what use are rats?' He replied, 'There is nothing in the world which does not exist for a very good reason. If there were no rats, snakes would destroy both the world and human beings, for rats eat the snake's eggs and destroy them. If this were not so, snakes would overrun the whole world.' The students then bowed and became his disciples. He then told them the following story:

The Chosen of God, Muḥammad (blessings and peace be upon him!) was sitting one day in the *miḥrāb* of the mosque at Qubā' and with him were his noble companions (may God be pleased with them!). Just then, a snake crawled quietly in through the door and hid itself under the Messenger's robe. 'Messenger of God,' said the snake, 'I am fleeing from an enemy; since you are the refuge of the two worlds, protect me!' Then, following the snake, there came in a hedgehog who likewise addressed Muḥammad. 'Messenger,' she said, 'give me my prey, for I have my children to look after.' So Muḥammad commanded them to give the hedgehog some offal, and with that she went away quite satisfied.

The Messenger then ordered the snake to be on its way since its enemy had turned round and gone out; but the snake said: 'I also have certain talents: let me show you, and then I shall go.' It then wrapped itself in a circle around the waist of the Messenger, just like a belt, intending to sting him without any mercy. He, however, put his blessed finger in the way so that the snake could only sting one of the joints. But when the snake drew back its head to bite, Abū Hureira opened a bag, and from it there sprang a black cat who tore the snake to pieces with his claws, and then stalked proudly to the Messenger. At that moment the latter said: 'Love of cats is part of faith: show love, though it be to a cat!' Then he passed his blessed hand over its back, and the blessing that came from his hand was such that even if you throw down a cat from a high roof, it is certain to land on its feet and its back will never touch the ground.

It is said that Abū Hureira raised twenty or thirty cats in his house, and to anyone who asked for a cat, he would give them one in gratitude, but keep a kitten from the litter for himself.

NANNAN

The Fleas' Flight

There is a village in Connacht which is famed for the church of Saint Nannan. Here, from ancient times, there was such a host of fleas that the place was virtually deserted on account of the pestilence and was left empty of inhabitants. But then, through the intercession of Saint Nannan, the fleas were banished to a nearby meadow. So great were the merits of the saint that the divine power cleansed the place so thoroughly that not a single one could afterwards be found there. But in the meadow, there was such a superabundance of fleas that for ever afterwards it remained inaccessible, not only to people but even to beasts.

NŪRĪ

Instruction in Meditation

Shiblī told this story: 'I went to visit Nūrī and found him sitting in meditation: not a single one of his hairs was moving. I said to him: "From whom did you learn such good control?" "From a cat over a mousehole," he replied, "but he was more motionless than I am." '

OWAIN AP CARADOG AP IESTYN

A Dog's Devotion

Owain ap Caradog ap Iestyn once owned a large and beautiful greyhound with streaks of different colours in its coat. On one occasion, when it was defending its master, it was pierced by arrows and spears and suffered seven wounds, but not before it had mangled many of its master's enemies and assassins with its teeth. After its wounds were newly healed, the dog was sent by William, earl of Gloucester, to Henry II, the king of the English, as evidence of such an extraordinary feat.

There is no beast which loves or recognises a person more than a dog, and sometimes, if its owner dies, the dog refuses to go on living. For the sake of its owner, it is not afraid to face the dangers of death. A dog, therefore, is ready to die for its owners and to die with its owners. So I do not think it would be out of place to insert here an example of this adduced by Suetonius in his work *On the Nature of Animals* and by Ambrose in his *Hexameron*:

At dusk, in a remote part of the city of Antioch, a man who was accompanied by his dog was murdered. The person responsible for his death was a soldier intent on robbery, and he escaped into another part of the city under cover of early darkness. Where the corpse lay unburied, a large crowd of onlookers gathered; and the dog, whining and howling, lamented the calamity which had befallen its master. The soldier who had killed him then came along, as if by chance, intending to prove his innocence (with the low cunning of the human race) by mingling with the crowd as if he were on duty. He therefore joined the throng of people who were standing round and went up to the body as if moved by compassion. Then, for a moment, the dog ceased its sorrowing and grieving, assumed the arms of revenge, and seized the man and held him fast.

As it did so, it howled in so piteous a manner that everyone there was moved to tears. That the dog seized him alone from among so many and refused to let him go was taken as proof of his guilt: particularly since the allegation of the crime could not simply be attributed to the dog hating him or being jealous of him or having been maltreated by him. So because he was so strongly suspected of being the murderer (which he, of course, continually denied) it was decided to test the truth of the matter by combat. The parties therefore met in a field with a great crowd of people standing round: the dog on one side, armed only with its teeth, and the soldier on the other, wielding a stick about a yard long. Eventually the dog was victorious and overcame the murderer; and after he had yielded, he suffered an ignominious end on the public gallows.

PAUL THE GREEK

The Recalcitrant Lion

Abba Alexander of the monastery of Calamon, just by the holy Jordan, told this tale: At one time when we were with abba Paul the Greek in his cave, someone came along and knocked on the door and the old man went out and opened it for him. He then fetched some bread and soaked pulse, put them in front of him, and he ate them. I assumed that it was some stranger, but when I glanced out of the window, I saw that it was actually a lion.

I said to the old man: 'Venerable Sir, why did you feed him? Tell me the reason.' He said to me: 'I exhorted him not to injure people or animals, and I said: "Come each day, and I shall provide you with your food." And see, he has now been coming here twice a day for seven months and I give him his food.'

A few days later I went back to him, wanting to buy some wine flasks from him, and said: 'What is it, venerable sir? How is the lion?' 'In a bad way,' he replied. 'Why?' I asked him. He said to me: 'He came here yesterday so that I could feed him and I saw that his chin was stained with blood. "What's this?" I said to him, "You have disobeyed me and have eaten flesh! By the blessed Lord, you flesh-eater, I shall no longer give you the food of the fathers! Get away from here!" But he did not want to go. Then I took a rope, looped it back on itself three times, and gave him three blows. Then he went away.'

PINCHAS HURWITZ OF FRANKFURT

A Horse's Claim to Heaven

Once upon a time, on a harsh winter's night, a man was passing through the little town of Lakhovitch where Rabbi Pinchas, the *Hafla'ah*, occupied the position of rabbi. The man was bitterly cold and had undergone a great deal, and was eager to find a house so that he could go in and get warm. To his joy he saw in the distance a little house with light shining from the window: it was, in fact, the dwelling of the *Hafla'ah* who, at that time, was pronouncing the lament over Jerusalem. The man, who would soon have been frozen stiff, knocked on the rabbi's window and asked to come in. The rabbi hurried to open the door for the man, gave him food and drink, and prepared a place for him to sleep for the night.

The man then thought to himself: 'What comfort the rabbi has: he sits in a warm room and wants for nothing, while I, day and night, must be on the road to earn my daily bread.' And he asked the rabbi: 'This world is a bitter place for me: I have to work hard to earn my living. Will I at least have a share in the World to Come?' The rabbi was annoyed at the man's complaint against Providence and retorted: 'Come now! On your argument, doesn't your horse have a better claim to the World to Come? You at least have found your way into a warm room, but your horse, a creature of God like yourself and who works even harder than you do, is now standing outside, uncomplaining in the bitter cold, ready to go wherever you want!'

PISENTIUS OF QIFT

Like Mother, Like Son

One day, our father the holy Pisentius went to a village to visit the church, and after he had attended to the congregation he went back to his monastery. As he was walking along

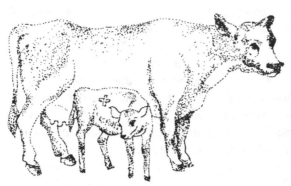

the path by the irrigation canal, one of the peasants brought a cow he owned to him so that he could make the sign of the cross on it. Now behold the power of God and you will be amazed! The cross which the holy man made with his finger on the belly of the cow penetrated into her as far as her infant! And this is proved by the fact that when she gave birth they found the cross which the holy man had marked on her from the outside clearly visible, as white in its whiteness as wool or snow, on the little calf she brought forth.

POEMEN

Keeping Warm in Winter

Abba Agathonicus, superior of the monastery of Kastellion of our holy father Sabas used to tell this tale: 'I went down to Rouba one day to visit abba Poemen the Grass-Eater, and when I had found him I told him my thoughts. When it was evening, he sent me into a cave; but because it was winter and the night was bitterly cold, I was chilled to the bone. Early next morning the old man came to me and said: "What's the matter, my son?" I said to him: "Forgive me, father, but I have had a terrible night because of the cold". "Is that so, my son?", he said to me, "I did not feel the cold". And I was amazed at hearing this since he was stark naked. So I said to him: "Of

your charity, tell me how you were not cold!" He said: "A lion
came along and went to sleep beside me, and it was he who
kept me warm. Yet I tell you this, brother: I am doomed to be
eaten by the beasts". "Why?" I asked him. "When I was living
in my own country", he said (he came from the two Galatias),
"I was a shepherd of sheep; but I ignored a passing stranger
and my dogs ate him. I could have saved him, but I did not;
instead, I did not interfere, and the dogs killed him. And I
know that I, too, must die in the same way". Three years later,
just as the old man had said, he was devoured by wild beasts.'

RŪMĪ

The Ass's Bray

One day in the community our Master the blessed
Jalāl-ud-Dīn Rūmī uttered these thoughts and words: 'God
the Truth (may
He be glorified!)
has said in the
glorious Qur'ān:
"The harshest of
all voices is the
voice of the ass"
(Qur'ān 31:19).
What this means
is that among the
animals it is the ass
which is credited

with the harshest and most disagreeable voice; but do my
friends know the significance of this?' The friends bowed and
entreated an explanation.

'All the animals,' he said, 'have a cry, a yearning call, a
particular way of showing thanks, with which they glorify their

Creator and Provider. The camel has its grumbling; the lion its roar; the deer its bleat; the fly its buzz; the bee its hum; and so on. In heaven, likewise, the angels and other spiritual beings have their hymns; and human beings, too, have their professions of faith and various devout feelings and expressions, both inward and outward. The poor ass, however, brays on two occasions only: when it wants sex or when it wants food, just as the poet says:

> It is like the wicked ass: if you fill it full, it kicks you; and if it is hungry, it brays.

The ass, therefore, is continually the slave of its genitals or its gullet; but in the same way, if anyone does not have in his soul a desire for submission to God and a passionate love for Him, and has not in his head a desire for Him or a secret, then as far as God is concerned, they are less than an ass: 'They are like cattle: indeed, they are even more astray!' (Qur'ān 7:179).

> Know that concupiscence is an ass: but to submit to it is still more shameful;
> If you do not know the way, see what the ass wants and do the opposite: that is the right path.'

It happened one day that our Master, together with all the friends, was riding on an ass on his way to the country estate of Ḥusām-ud-Dīn Chelebī. 'The ass,' he said, 'is the mount of the righteous. Even some of the prophets have been served in this way: Seth and Ezra and Jesus the Messiah, just as our Messenger Muḥammad (peace be upon him!).' The friend and theologian Shihāb-ud-Dīn, who was also mounted on an ass, then recited the following verse:

> Mount an ass without a saddle, blabbermouth!
> No ass is bare backed since the Messenger of God rode upon it!

But suddenly the ass of Shihāb-ud-Dīn began to bray and he, being angry with it, hit it on the head a number of times. 'Why are you hitting the poor beast?', said our Master. 'Don't you realise that it is she who is carrying you: that you are on top and she is underneath? What would you have done if the opposite had been the case? Truly, her braying stems from only one of two sources, her gullet or her genitals, and in both cases all creatures are alike. You should therefore mistreat everybody and hit them all over the head!' Shihāb-ud-Dīn, wholly repentant, dismounted from his ass, kissed her hoof, and caressed her.

Canine Initiates

[One day, Jalāl-ud-Dīn had gone to the bazaar—the local market-place and meeting place—in order to teach, and all the people of Konya gathered around him. He then 'turned away his blessed face from created beings to the wall' and began to teach them that esoteric and initiatory knowledge which in Arabic (and Persian) is called *ma'rifa* (most writers translate it as *gnosis*). But he continued so long with his discourse that the people gradually began to wander off, and by nightfall, at the time of the evening prayer, only the dogs of the market-place were left, and they had formed a circle around him:]

He turned his blessed gaze upon them and continued his explanations. The dogs nodded their heads and wagged their tails and whined very quietly. 'I swear by God,' said our

Master, 'the All-Highest, the Strongest, the Almighty, who alone is strong and mighty, that these dogs understand our esoteric teaching! Hereafter they shall no longer be called dogs, for they are of the family of that dog who sleeps with the Seven Sleepers in the cave.'

'Greater Love Hath No Cat...'

When he was getting ready to pass from this world, our Master spoke to no-one for three nights and days, nor would he permit anyone to speak to him. The Master's wife came before him, bowed, and asked the reason for his condition and this restriction. 'I am thinking about death,' he said, 'what will it be like?' Then, after reciting a verse, a cry came from his breast, he raised himself up, and remained unconscious for some hours.

But even in these last days he took thought for his blessed community, uttering cries and great sighs. There was a cat there who came to him, also uttering plaintive cries and  lamentations. Our Master smiled and said: 'Do you know what this poor cat is saying?' 'No,' they said. 'He is saying this,' said the Master. 'In these days you must depart for the Glorious Kingdom: you are returning to your original place. But me, poor cat that I am, what shall I do?' All the friends cried out and fainted away.

After the death of the Master, the cat remained without water or food for seven nights and days, and then it too died. Meleke-Khatūn, the Master's daughter, wrapped it in a shroud and buried it near our Master's own blessed tomb.

SERGIUS THE ANCHORITE

Leonine Communion

Some of the fathers of Sinai told us a story about abba
Sergius the anchorite, saying: When he was staying on Sinai,
the steward had put him in charge of the mules. But on one occasion, when he was going somewhere, there was a lion lying
across the road. When the mules and muleteers saw the lion,
they were filled with fear and retreated. Then abba Sergius
took a piece of blessed bread from his wallet, went up to the
lion and said to him: 'Take this blessed bread of the fathers and
go your way so that we can pass by'. And taking the
bread, the lion went away.

SHENOUTE THE GREAT

A Mother's Duty

One day, some men
brought to our father apa
Shenoute a camel who
had given birth. Her foal
was following her, but it
was very feeble because
its mother would never let
it take suck of her breast.
When our father saw her,
he brought a little water
from the basin in the
church and gave it to her,

and she drank it. He then put her son under her and said:
'If you will not accept your son, why ever did you give him
birth?' Straightaway she gave him milk without any trouble.
After this, her owners took her and returned to their home
glorifying God and our holy father apa Shenoute.

SUFYĀN AL-THAURI

Compassion

In the following story we find an example of the compassion which Sufyān showed to God's creatures. One day
when he was in the bazaar, he saw a little bird in a cage, flut-
tering and crying out. He bought it and set it free. Then, every
night, the little bird would come to Sufyān's house and watch
the whole night while Sufyān prayed, perching on him from
time to time.

When Sufyān died and was being carried to his grave,
that little bird joined the funeral procession, crying out with
the other mourners; and when Sufyān was committed to the
earth, the little bird dashed itself to the ground. Then a voice
came from the tomb: 'God Most High has forgiven Sufyān for
the compassion he had upon His creatures.' That little bird also
died and joined Sufyān (may the mercy of God be upon him!).

SYMEON THE ELDER

Guiding the Travellers

Some Jews were travelling on business to one of the
fortresses lying outside the region in which they lived when
there was a torrential downpour and a violent storm. Since
they were unable to see in front of them, they lost their way
and wandered in the desert, finding no village, no cave, and no
traveller. They were as storm-tossed on dry land as those on a
ship at sea. But then, as if coming to a harbour, they happened
upon the cave of the holy Symeon. There they saw a man covered in dirt and filth and wearing over his shoulders a small
ragged goat-skin. As soon as he saw them he greeted them
(for he was very courteous) and asked the reason for their visit.
They told him what had happened and implored him to point
out to them the road leading to the fortress. 'Wait,' he said,
'and straightaway I shall provide you with guides who will
show you the road you want.' They did as they were told,
therefore, and rested for a while. As they were sitting there,

along came two lions, not looking terrible, but fawning on
Symeon as on their master and showing their submission. With
a gesture, he commanded them to escort the men and lead
them to the road which they had left when they wandered
from their way.

The Ascetic and the Lion

[Symeon later decided to make a pilgrimage to Mount Sinai and, together with a number of like-minded companions, set out on the journey. When they came to the wilderness of Sodom, south of the Dead Sea, they were astonished to see a small hole in the ground from which protruded two arms, raised to heaven in prayer. When they came nearer the arms disappeared, and they discovered that down in the hole lived an ascetic who had also at one time intended to go on pilgrimage to Sinai. He had set out with a friend and they had sworn an oath to each other that not even death would put an end to their fellowship. Thus, said the ascetic, when it happened that his friend died in that very place, he buried him there, and by the side of his grave dug a second sepulchre in which he now dwelt and in which he awaited the end of his days. 'But,' said he, 'for my food I have dates which, on the instruction of my Protector, a certain brother brings to me.' Theodoret of Cyrrhus now takes up the story:]

As he was speaking, there appeared in the distance a lion. Symeon's companions were terrified, but when the ascetic who was sitting by the grave noticed it, he stood up and gestured to the lion to come round to the other side. It obeyed immediately and came up to them, carrying a bunch of dates. It then turned and went off again, and when it was a good distance from the men it lay down and went to sleep. The ascetic shared out the dates among them all and joined with them in praying and singing psalms; and at dawn, after they had finished their worship, he took leave of them and sent them on their way in amazement at this novel spectacle.

TATHAN

Tathan and His Pet Doves

The blessed Tathan had two tame doves who used to fly down and play on the table, and he found it relaxing to watch them and listen to their cooings. One day, when they were flying between the refectory
and the church, a kite
captured one of them,
and the clerics who
saw her captured told
the master about the
capture. He was sad-
dened when he heard
of it, but hoped that
through the power
of God she would be
restored to him.

Next day, when he came to the guest-house after the celebration of Mass, the rapacious kite flew down, holding the dove in his claws, and put her back, safe and sound, at the feet of the most holy teacher. When he saw her he was delighted, and said:

> Here is the dove which was dead: she is now alive again;
> She flies and plays: her breast preserved from any wound;
> I praise the Creator: such comfort he bestows upon his ser-
> vant;
> He has given back this bird: he has sent it to me by the
> wings of a kite.

Of Pigs and Piglets, Wolves and Cubs

One day a swineherd came to his master, the most de-vout Tathan, full of complaints about the loss of his piglets. Af-ter he had arrived, his master asked him what he wanted and what had happened to him. He answered Tathan, though he was very much afraid that the words he uttered would anger him: 'During this week (he said), a most fierce she-wolf visited my herd of pigs and carried off the piglets of one of the sows. Of the seven which were alive, there is none today. I follow this greedy wolf. She goes into a cave. I can't stop her. And so she feeds her own cubs with the flesh of my piglets. I am grieved about it. Now help me on account of my grief.'

When Tathan heard this, he answered the complaints of the swineherd and said: 'Faithful servant, go and grieve no more; for by my prayer God will pacify the fierceness of the wolf and she will injure you no more as she has injured you in the past.'

The swineherd, therefore, went back happily to his herd and early the next day he saw the wolf coming towards him and carrying in her mouth her own cub. At the door she released what she was carrying as if she did not own it, and then, tamed, and not as a wild animal, she went back to the forest. By divine power, the cub which she had left came straightaway to the childless sow, sucking on her teats, and staying with her as if she were its own mother.

Nourished in this way it grew up like a house-dog, not like a wolf, and guarded the forests. For a period of three years neither beast nor robber injured the herd. At the end of the third year, it visited the dwelling of its master Tathan as it used to do every day, but a servant, for some reason which displeased him, hit the wolf on its side. Struck and offended, it turned round three times and went back to the wood; and because of its anger and indignation it never again returned to the herd. This was how the she-wolf restored the piglet to the venerable Tathan. Has anyone heard of a more marvellous miracle?

THEON

Theon's Friends

[Theon had a cell not far from Oxyrhynchus where he had practised silence for thirty years. He was a healer, a miracle-worker, and a clairvoyant. He spoke only once, and that was when some robbers had tried to plunder his cave. He had prayed, and they had remained rooted to the spot. Next day, a crowd of Theon's devotees arrived at his cell and proposed burning the thieves. 'Let them go', he said, 'otherwise the gift of healing will leave me.'
On other occasions, if he needed to communicate, he wrote on a slate in Greek, Latin, or Coptic, as the circumstances demanded. His diet consisted of uncooked vegetables.]

They say that he would go out of his cell at night and keep company with the wild animals, and would give them to drink from whatever water he had. One could certainly see tracks of antelopes and wild asses and gazelles and other creatures around his hermitage, for they always delighted him.

WERBURGA OF CHESTER

A Goose Dinner

I shall now narrate a miracle of the holy Werburga which was so celebrated that it earned her renown among those that lived there and was long remembered. She had a farm outside the walls of Chester, and the wild geese used to come there and eat the corn. The estate manager, whose job it was, made every effort to drive them off, but to little effect. So when he came to wait upon his mistress, he complained of this matter in his report of the other events of the day. 'Go', she said, 'and shut them all up in the hut.' The countryman was astonished at this strange order and thought the lady was joking. But when he realised she was insistent and in earnest, he went back to the cornfield where he had first noticed the unruly marauders and in a loud voice informed them that they were to follow him in accordance with their mistress's command. Then all of them flocked together, and with their necks drooping they followed their enemy and were shut up in the

hut. But since the countryman had no fear that there was anyone there to accuse him, he presumed to have one of them for his dinner.

At daybreak the maiden Werburga arrived, and after scolding the birds for plundering other people's property, she told them to take flight. But because they knew that their number was not complete, they did not lack the sense to circle round the lady's feet, refusing to go away; and by complaining to her in whatever way they could, they aroused the maiden's compassion. By God's revelation she understood that the birds were not complaining for nothing, and after diligently questioning the manager, learned of the theft. She ordered him to collect the bones and bring them to her. And there and then, at a healing sign from the maiden's hand, skin and flesh covered the bones, and feathers began to grow on the skin; and eventually the living bird, at first hopping briskly but soon flying, launched itself into the air. The others, their number now complete, had no hesitation in following, but only after they had first showed their reverence for their deliverer. The merits of this maiden, therefore, are proclaimed at Chester and her miracles extolled.

WULFSTAN OF WORCESTER

Why No-One Should Ever Wear Catskin

[Wulfstan was known for the austerity of his life and his dedication to God. In a world where elaborate eating and heavy drinking were the norm he would remain temperate, though he would always provide an abundance of food and drink for those that visited him. Similarly, although he employed a body-guard of knights in accordance with the Norman practice of the time, he was himself a humble man. He loved to repeat verses from the psalms and was assiduous in his attendance at the Divine Offices; but since he himself was always so scrupulous, he had no patience at all with those who were not. If any were late for matins 'through drunkenness or sleepiness', he would give them stinging blows with his cane. His dress was sober and he eschewed ostentation, even of the cheapest sort, as this anecdote demonstrates:]

He was quite unconcerned about wearing the cheaper varieties of clothes, and preferred to keep out the cold with the fleeces of sheep rather than with other kinds of skins. And if anyone said to him that he might at least clothe himself in catskin, he would reply with joking courtesy: 'Believe me (for this way of swearing had become a habit with the bishop), I have heard of people singing the *Agnus Dei*, "O Lamb of God", but never the *Cattus Dei*, "O Cat of God"; so I would rather be warmed by a lamb than by a cat.' The fear of the Lord had become so firmly fixed in his mind that what others would turn into ostentation, he would change into the stuff of compunction.

ZEV WOLF OF ZBARAZH

Simple Service

On one occasion, Rabbi Wolf, 'the Simple', was travelling to a nearby village to be present at a circumcision. It was a viciously cold day in December, but he could not refuse the villager's invitation. And when the people from the surrounding area heard that the rabbi would be coming, they all hurried to the village and prepared a great feast in his honour.

When the meal was over and the rabbi had finished his after-dinner speech, the thought came to him that the driver

of his horse and cart was outside in the cold. He therefore crept out of the house unobtrusively and said to the driver: 'My son, you are cold: go into the room and warm yourself for a while.' The driver answered: 'How can I leave the cart and horse untended?' But the rabbi persisted and said: 'I will stay with the horse and cart until you have warmed yourself and come back out again.' The man obeyed, but once he was in the room, he was in no hurry to go out again into the icy cold.

Meanwhile, the *hasidim* were waiting for the rabbi, but when they realised that he had disappeared without saying the grace after the meal, they went out to look for him. They found him, his limbs shaking with cold, walking up and down by the horse and cart. In amazement they asked him: 'Rabbi, what are you doing here?' Then said the rabbi in his simplicity: 'I came out to send the driver into the room so that he could warm himself a little. I stayed here to look after the horse and cart.'

PART II
THE PEOPLE

AN INTRODUCTORY TALE

This story comes from the 'Book of the Animals', the 'Llibre de les Bèsties', of the Catalan mystic Ramon Llull. Llull was born in Mallorca probably between 1232 and 1235 and until his conversion at the age of thirty led a fashionable life of pleasure and indolence. After his conversion, however, he became a Franciscan Tertiary and devoted himself to the conversion of the Moors. His literary output was immense (he wrote in Catalan, Latin, and Arabic) and at some date between 1286 and 1294 he composed the *Llibre de Meravelles o Fèlix*. This is a lengthy, rambling work, a sort of companion-volume to the more impressive *Blanquerna*, and the most interesting section of it is undoubtedly the seventh book, the 'Llibre de les Bèsties'. Much of this seventh section is derived from Arabic sources, but Llull has transformed the material into a text very much his own. Llull died a martyr's death in North Africa in about 1315 (it was his third missionary journey to the Moors): he walked the streets, loudly proclaiming the truths (as he maintained) of the Christian religion, and a crowd began to gather and follow him, gradually becoming more and more hostile. Eventually stones and rocks were thrown, and it was not long before 'the Fool of Love' was dead.

For the Catalan text of the story I have used the edition of Père Bohigas (which also contains a useful brief introduction), *Ramon Llull: Llibre de les Bèsties* (Antologia Catalana 1; Barcelona, 1983 [eighth edition]) 34–5.

Notes

Llull's text has very few temporal indicators, and I have been fairly free in adding 'then,' 'later,' 'at the same time,' and so on.

wicked, powerful, and crafty] the word for 'crafty' is *maestre* (*mestre* in modern Catalan) and it means 'skilled, masterful, expert, subtle, ingenious, and crafty'.

AN ANONYMOUS MONK OF THE LAVRA OF ABBA PETER

The identity of this monk is unknown, but his lavra, that of abba Peter, was one of a group of five communities lying just about midway between Jericho and the northern tip of the Dead Sea. It was about a mile and a half from the banks of the Jordan.

A somewhat similar story appears in the *Kashf al-Mahjūb* of 'Alī ibn 'Uthmān al-Hujwīrī: one day a seeker after knowledge, Ibrahim ar-Raqqī, went to visit Muslim al-Maghribī (a spiritual teacher who died about the year 900) and found him giving instruction in the mosque. But because he pronounced certain Arabic words incorrectly, the seeker lost faith in the teacher, left the mosque, and planned to go home. Next day, when he was going down to the river Euphrates to perform the ablutions before prayer, he came upon a lion sleeping

on the road. He turned round to flee, but was faced with another lion which had been tracking him. He cried out in terror,
and Muslim, who heard the cry, came out of his cell to see
what was happening. When the lions saw him, they prostrated
themselves in front of him, and he fondled their ears and said:
'You dogs of God, haven't I told you that you mustn't interfere
with my guests?' Then he said to Ibrahim, 'You have spent
your time trying to correct what is external for the sake of
God's creatures, and it follows that you are afraid of them. I
have spent my time in correcting what is internal for the sake
of God, and it follows that they are afraid of me.' The Greek
text of the story of the anonymous monk is to be found in *caput* 18 of the *Pratum Spirituale* of John Moschus, PL 87: 2865A.

AN ANONYMOUS MONK OF FONDI

Fondi is an important city and diocese in Central Italy,
and the monastery of Fondi referred to here is the monastery
of St Magnus, founded in the mid-fifth century by Honoratus
(who is now the patron of the town). According to Gregory
the Great (whose *Dialogues* are our main source of information about the monastery and its abbots) Honoratus was the
superior of some two hundred monks and was a source of
inspiration and edification for the whole area. When he died
at the beginning of the sixth century, he was succeeded by
an unnamed abbot whose prior was Libertinus, a disciple of
Honoratus, and a story about Libertinus and a horse will be
found below in its proper place.

The Latin text of this tale is to be found in Gregory the
Great, *Liber Dialogorum* I.3; PL 77: 164B–5A.

We might note that snakes are not always so obedient,
nor so fortunate. In most of the tales in which they appear,
the saints are primarily interested in getting rid of them. Later
in the *Dialogues*, for example, we hear of a deacon who had

come to visit Florentius (there is a story about him and his
bear in its proper place) and was terrified to see that the area
round his hermitage was infested with serpents. 'Servant of
God', he screamed, 'pray for me!' Florentius came out of his
cell and prayed to God to deal with the infestation. There was
an immediate explosion of thunder and all the snakes were
struck dead on the spot. But Florentius had not yet finished.
Looking at the multitude of corpses he again spoke to God:
'Now you've killed them', he said, 'who's going to get rid of
the bodies?' Straightaway there appeared a flock of birds who
flew down on the corpses, picked them up, and flew off again.
And from that moment the region round the hermitage of Florentius was entirely free of snakes. (The tale is to be found in
Book III, section 15 of the *Dialogues*).

TWO ANONYMOUS MONKS IN EGYPT

Both these stories are to be found in the first *Dialogue*
of Sulpicius Severus. Sulpicius, who was born about 363 and
died in the early 420's, was the author of an admirable *Historia
Sacra*, narrating major events from the Creation to his own day,
and the popular, famous, and credulous *Life of Saint Martin
of Tours*. His three *Dialogues* (which date from about 405) are
not so well known, but the first of them has some interesting
things to say about Egyptian monasticism. The narrator is not
Sulpicius, but his friend Postumianus who has just returned
from a three-year visit to the east.

The Latin text of 'The desert in bloom' is to be found
in PL 20: 191D–2C (*Dialogue* I, xiii [abridged]), and that of
'Penitence' in PL 20: 192C–3B (*Dialogue* I, xiv).

BARTHOLOMEW OF FARNE

Bartholomew was born at Whitby of Scandinavian parents. His early life was somewhat dissolute, but after undergoing a conversion, he went to Norway where he was ordained a priest. He then returned to England, spent some three years in parish work, and then, in the 1140s, became a monk at Durham. Soon afterwards he retired as a hermit to the island of Inner Farne (a wild, wind-swept, rocky, and deserted place: the home of sea-birds and seals) where he spent the remaining forty-two years of his life. Bartholomew, it seems, did not much care for people, though he was always generous to the many visitors who came to see him. He preferred the company of his pet bird and, all things considered, his choice of  the eremitic life was probably the best thing both for him and for everyone else as well. He died in 1193 and his feast-day is 24 June.

Both stories are taken from the life of Bartholomew by Geoffrey of Durham in T. Arnold (ed.), *Symeonis Dunelmensis Opera* (Rolls Series 75/1; London, 1882). For 'Prey and Predator', see page 311 (section 19), and for 'Bartholomew to the Rescue', see pages 315–6 (sections 24–5).

Notes

Bartholomew To the Rescue

certain birds] these are the eider-ducks of Farne. They are beautiful creatures, especially the male, who is snowy white on top and deep velvet black underneath. The female normally lays between four and ten eggs. The Farne islands are still home to an astonishing variety of avian life and are now (rightly) a bird sanctuary.

BENEDICT OF NURSIA

Benedict was the true father of western monasticism, but the greatness of his renown lies in stark contrast to the paucity of sources on his life and character. The second book of Gregory the Great's *Dialogues* is virtually all that we have. But on the other hand, Benedict's great achievement is not to be found in what he did or how he lived or the miracles he may or may not have performed; it is to be found instead in his Rule, and this is obviously not the place to discuss the astonishing influence of that remarkable document. Benedict himself was born at Nursia about 480, and after being trained in Rome, left the Eternal City to become a hermit at Subiaco on the River Anio. Here he attracted a number of disciples and it was from here that he went to act as superior at the monastery at Vicovaro, about twenty miles further down the river. The local clergy, however, were quite possibly just as jealous as Gregory describes them, and it is equally possible that an attempt really was made to have the saint poisoned. At all events, he found Vicovaro unsatisfactory, and about 525 moved to Monte Cassino, near Naples, where he settled permanently, where he wrote the final version of his Rule, and where he died about 550. His feast-day was formerly 21 March, but is now celebrated by the Roman Church on 11 July.

The Latin text of the story is to be found in Gregory the Great, *Liber Dialogorum* II,8; PL 66: 148BC.

BENNO OF MEISSEN

According to tradition (which may not be correct)
Benno was born in 1010 at Hildesheim and was educated by
Saint Bernward, bishop of Hildesheim, who was also one of his
relatives. In due course, he was consecrated bishop of Meissen
and, if we are to believe his biographers, was an exemplary
prelate. He was himself devout, generous, and ascetic, and
did his best to encourage these virtues in his clergy. He also
restored the public singing of the Divine Offices, and his own
love of good music presumably contributed to his rebuke of
the frog. On the other hand, I have known some frogs who had
better voices than some of my friends. Benno became involved

in the bitter struggle between
Pope Gregory VII and Henry
IV on the question of investi-
tures, and, as a consequence of
his involvement, not only spent
a year in prison, but in 1085
was deposed from his bishopric
because of his support for the
pope. Three years later, however, the political climate
changed and he was able to regain his see. He remained there
as bishop of Meissen until his death in about 1106. His feast-
day is 16 June.

The Latin text of the story is to be found in chapter 54
of the late life by Jerome Emser, *Acta Sanctorum* IV: 139 col.
2DE (June 16).

A similar story is told of Rūmī (q.v.) by Aflākī. He
tells us that it was the Master's custom to go each year with
his friends and companions to the thermal baths at Ilghin near
Konya where they would stay for six or seven weeks. On one
occasion, when his disciples were sitting in a circle at the side
of one of the pools and Rūmī was delivering a discourse, all
the frogs in the pool decided to croak at the same time.

'What's all this racket?', shouted the Master, 'Will you speak or shall I?' They immediately ceased their croaking and were silent for as long as his sermon lasted. When he had finished, he went to the edge of the pool and made a sign as if to say: 'All right, now you can croak again', and they immediately resumed their chatter. We shall see a little later that Saint Canice had a similar problem with noisy sea-birds. There is, incidentally, a *ḥadīth*, a tradition, of Muḥammad which prohibits the faithful from killing frogs. Why? Because when the Throne of God was upon the waters, the frogs were nearest to it, and all their croaking was in God's praise.

Notes

all the frogs in Seraphus are dumb] Seraphus or Serifos is one of the Cyclades, a small island in the Aegean Sea south-west of Syros. Emser's source is here Book VIII section lxxxiii of Pliny's *Natural History*. Pliny does not tell us why the frogs are mute, but he says that if they are removed from the island, they all start croaking again.

BERNARD OF CLAIRVAUX

Bernard was born of a noble family at Fontaines, near Dijon, in 1090. He was known for his charm and eloquence, but early in his life showed a marked preference for the monastic profession. This found its fulfilment in 1113 when Bernard, together with some thirty other noble companions (Bernard was nothing if not persuasive), entered the monastery of Cîteaux, which was then in a state of rapid decay. Indeed, the Bernardine influx appears to have saved it from certain extinction. Two years later, however, he left Cîteaux to be abbot of the new foundation of Clairvaux; and under his charismatic leadership the new monastery became the real centre of the Order. Despite his obvious predilection for the monastic life, Bernard was deeply involved in affairs of church and state: he was instrumental in gaining recognition for the Knights Templar; he was much involved in the papal struggle which resulted in the recognition of Innocent II; he attacked the ideas of every heretic he could; he intervened in episcopal elections right, left, and centre; and he preached (with extreme vehemence) the Second Crusade (which fortunately failed). He could be passionate, ascetic, impetuous, bigoted, saintly, interfering, generous, petty, persuasive, pleasant, and unpleasant. His writings reveal much of great beauty and undoubted power; his intellectual accomplishments have, in my view, been overestimated. If medieval France had been present-day Iran, Bernard would have made a splendid ayatollah. He died in 1153 and was canonized in 1174. His feast-day is 20 August.

The Latin texts of both stories are to be found in the *Vita Prima Sancti Bernardi* written by Bernard's friend (and intellectual superior) William of Saint-Thierry: the Foigny flies appear in *Vita prima* xi.52 (PL 185: 256BC) and the story of the horse in *ibid.*, xiii.66 (PL 185: 263D–4A).

Notes

The Flies of Foigny

Foigny] Foigny was founded by Bernard in 1121 and is situated (as William says) in the diocese of Laon. It is actually about seven miles north-east of Vervins. The date of the dedication of the church (and hence of the demise of the flies) was 11 November 1124. The story has, of course, major theological overtones: if flies can be excommunicated, it implies that they were formerly communicants, a point of view which most Christians would be loathe to accept.

BLAISE

Blaise is said to have been the son of rich and noble Christians, but early in his life (as is befitting a future saint) he showed a marked propensity for religion. He was consecrated bishop when he was still young, and after retreating to a hermitage and performing the various miracles narrated in this story, he was caught up in the Great Persecution, tortured, and finally beheaded in the early fourth century. None of this information, though traditional, is reliable, and the Lives of the saint (both in Greek and Latin) seem to be pure invention. Because of his association with the animals, Blaise is the patron saint of all wild creatures; because of his cure of the boy who was choking on the fish-bone, he is the patron of those who suffer from diseases of the throat; and because he was torn with wool-combs before being decapitated (a form of torture not uncommon in the martyrdoms), he is the patron of those involved in the wool trade. His feast-day is 3 February.

The Latin text of the account is to be found in T. Graesse (ed.), *Jacobi a Voragine, Legenda Aurea* (Vratislava, 1890 [third edition]; rpt. Osnabrück, 1969) 167–8.

Notes

Sebaste] Sebaste is the modern Sivis, a large, ancient, and important city located in central Turkey.

the persecution of Diocletian] the Great Persecution broke out in 303 and lasted for about nine years. It came to an end with Constantine's victory over Maxentius at the Battle of the Milvian Bridge (28 October 312).

the governor of the area] the *praeses* or *procurator*. He was the official responsible for the civil administration and the supervision of the imperial revenues and taxes.

BRENDAN THE VOYAGER

Brendan was born about 485, probably near Tralee, and after the usual education and training became a monk and, in due course, abbot of Clonfert, the famous monastery in Co. Galway which Brendan himself is said to have founded. He travelled extensively (as did many other Irish monks of the period), and tales are told of his visiting Scotland, Wales, and Brittany. More dramatic than these voyages, however, is the *Navigatio Sancti Brendani*, in which, according to many, we have an early account of a journey from Ireland to the Americas. Whether this is true or not is, of course, unknown, though some years ago Tim Severin demonstrated that it was certainly possible. But whether true or not, the story of the voyage was immensely popular and was translated into a considerable number of vernacular languages. According to the text of the *Navigatio*, Brendan returned safely home from wherever it was he got to, and died sometime between 577 and 583. His feast-day is 16 May (and he must be distinguished from his contemporary, Saint Brendan of Birr).

The Latin texts of 'Iasconius' and 'The True Nature of Birds' are to be found in C. Selmer (ed.), *Navigatio Sancti Brendani Abbatis* (Notre Dame, 1959) 20–21 (*cap.* 10) and 22–5 (*cap.* 11); that of 'A Diet of Fish' is in C. Plummer, *Vitae Sanctorum Hiberniae* (Oxford, 1910; rpt. 1968) I: 138 (*cap.* lxxv).

Notes

Iasconius

Iasconius] the name is derived from the Irish word for
fish: *iasc*.

The True Nature of Birds

We are from the ruin of
the Ancient Enemy . . .] what
the bird means here is that she
and her companions did not
actually join with Satan and
his companions in sinning,
but they did not speak out
against it either. The Paradise
of Birds, therefore, is rather like
limbo: a place where the avian
spirits enjoy the highest *natural*
happiness, but not the *super-
natural* felicity which is the lot of the blessed.

A Diet of Fish

a cat] or perhaps a 'mercat' or 'sea-cat' (the Latin has
murchat, but this might be a corruption of *muriceps*). The Irish
version of the story adds a gloss to the effect that this cat had
grown to the size of a young ox or a three-year old horse.

BRYNACH

Brynach (who must be distinguished from the better known and astonishingly prolific Brychan) appears to have been an Irishman who, after going on pilgrimage to Rome and residing in Brittany for some years, eventually made his way to Dyfed in South Wales, where, after many adventures (on one occasion he narrowly escaped assassination), he finally settled at Nevern on the banks of the Caman. He established a number of chapels or small monastic foundations (what the Latin life calls his *loca*) in South and Central Wales, and died, revered and respected, probably about 560.

The Latin text of the story is to be found in A. W. Wade-Evans, *Vitae Sanctorum Britanniae et Genealogiae* (Board of Celtic Studies, University of Wales History and Law Series, No.9; Cardiff, 1944) 10–12. We might note that the story of the resurrected cow is common to a number of saint's lives, but the version in the *Life of Brynach* is one of the most complete and the most lively.

Notes

The Wolf and the Resurrected Cow

Maelgwyn, the king of Wales] Maelgwyn Gwynedd, by all accounts a contemporary of Arthur, appears to have ruled much of North Wales from his seat in Degannwy. He was a charismatic, cunning, cruel, christian, and complex character, very tall and strong, who, at the height of his fame and fortune, withdrew to a monastery and then, shortly afterwards, left it again to resume his career of liberality and licentiousness, generosity and greed. His life is much more interesting than that of most saints, but this is not the place to tell it. He died about 547.

to be free from any obligation] i.e. Brynach did not intend to establish a precedent which could have unfortunate consequences in the future.

was very short tempered] *erat facilis a mentis tranquillitate moveri*: literally, 'he was easily moved from tranquillity of mind.'

BUITE

Buite (or Boetius in Latin) came from the region of Louth in Northern Ireland and, according to one ancient and respectable tradition, travelled as a youth to Wales where he was instructed by Saint Teilo of Llandaff, a most important figure in sixth-century Welsh ecclesiastical history. Another tradition, which has him travelling to Italy, most probably derives from a scribe misreading *Walia* (Wales) as *Italia* (Italy). Be that as it may, Buite certainly returned to Ireland where he founded the celebrated monastery of Mainistir-Buite, one of the oldest monastic foundations in the country, and, a short distance from it, a convent for nuns. He died in the year 521 and is commemorated on 7 December.

The Latin text of the story is to be found in Plummer, *Vitae Sanctorum Hiberniae* I: 90–91 (*cap.* xiii-xiv).

CANICE

Canice or Canicus (in Latin) or Cainnech (in Irish) or Kenneth (in English) was born about 520 in Co. Derry. He was probably trained at Clonard by Saint Finnian (though the Welsh sources would have him educated in Wales by Saint

Cadoc) and became a friend of the great Columba, whom he accompanied on one occasion to Inverness and whom he frequently visited on Iona. He certainly spent some time in Wales at Llancarvan (his own community in Ireland having been ravaged by plague), but soon returned to Ireland to found a number of monasteries, the most important being Aghaboe, 'The Field of the Ox,' in Ossory. He also had a cell at Kilkenny, and the city has taken its name from that of the saint. His attitude to animals is also exemplified by the grim penance he imposed upon a callous householder. One day, we are told, Canice came to the house of a rich man and there found a starving dog, hardly more than skin and bones. On enquiring whose duty it was to look after the animal, he was told that it was that of the rich man's wife. 'In that case,' said Saint Canice to the lady, 'until the end of the year you shall eat only what you gave to the dog, and you shall give to the dog what you yourself would normally eat.' There are dedications to Saint Canice in Ireland, Scotland (the best known being Inchkenneth in Mull), and Wales, and his feast day (which should obviously be celebrated by every S.P.C.A.) is 11 October. He died about 600, probably in his early eighties.

The Latin texts of both stories are to be found in Plummer, *Vitae Sanctorum Hiberniae* I: 161 (*cap.* xxv [the isle of birds]) and 165 (*cap.* xxxvi [the runaway lectern]).

CARANNOG

Carannog, Carantoc, or (in Breton) Caredec was an important figure in the evangelization of central Cornwall and northern Brittany, probably in the sixth century. There may, in fact, have been a group of saints involved in the enterprise, since dedications to Carannog, Petrog, Briog, Meugan, and Gwbert frequently occur in very close proximity. He is also said to have visited Ireland (where his name appears as Cairnech) and cooperated with Patrick and Benen/Benignus in missionary work in that country. That Carannog did visit Ireland is indeed probable; that he was associated with Patrick is out of the question. He had an extensive cult in South Wales, Cornwall, Somerset, and Brittany, and his feast day is 16 May. The tale which follows (which is also part of the Arthurian legend) has obvious similarities to the story of George and the dragon, but in the case of Carannog the dragon is not killed. Why should it be? Tame dragons are interesting to have around, and they are, in any case, an endangered species.

The Latin text of the story is to be found in Wade-Evans, *Vitae Sanctorum Britanniae et Genealogiae* (see above s.v. Brynach), 144–6.

Notes

Cadwy and Arthur] the King Arthur of the Arthurian legend and his co-ruler.

in that part of the country] i.e. in the region of South Wales, South-West England, and North and Central Cornwall.

Dindraithou] most probably the large hill-fort which the Irish sources call Dun Tradui and the Welsh sources Dindraethwy. It appears to have been situated somewhere in Cornwall, but the precise location is uncertain.

Carhampton] in the text the name of the place is given as *Carrum* or *Carrov*, and although Carhampton (in Somerset) is the most likely identification, Crantock in Cornwall has also been suggested.

where his altar had come to shore] this was a portable altar of indescribable colour which had been given to Carannog by Christ himself. When the saint was trying to decide where

to establish his monastery, he threw the altar into the River
Severn on the assumption that God would bring it safely to
land at the appropriate spot. There was nothing unusual in
this: Celtic saints frequently sailed around on their altars. It
was a well-established and economical mode of transport.

Off it went and remained in the neighbourhood as the
ordinance of God had earlier decreed] the Latin text is here
somewhat obscure.

CIARAN OF CLONMACNOISE

Ciaran was born about 512 in either Roscommon or
Westmeath. His father was most probably a cartwright, but the
effect of the gospel story on Ciaran's *Vita* has transformed him
into a carpenter. Ciaran later studied under Finnian, the famous abbot of Clonard, where he was one of that group
known to succeeding generations as the Twelve Apostles of
Ireland. He then spent some time on the islands of Aran and
Scattery before making his way to Clonmacnoise in what is
now Co. Meath. Here, on the banks of the River Shannon, he
founded the monastery which, in course of time, was to become one of the great centres of Irish learning. Ciaran himself
died young—the traditional accounts (again affected by the
gospels) tell us that he was only thirty-three—but the cause
of his untimely demise was not youthful frailty, but jealousy.
The other Irish *sancti*, we are told, were so envious of his accomplishments that all of them, with the exception of Columba,
fasted and prayed to God that Ciaran would die young. That
he appears to have done so is perhaps evidence for the power
of prayer and of the fact that God is no respecter of persons.
The date of his death was probably about 545 and he is commemorated on September 9.

The Latin text of the story is to be found in Plummer,
Vitae Sanctorum Hiberniae I: 202 (*cap.* v).

CIARAN OF SAIGHIR

Ciaran of Saighir, who must be distinguished from Ciaran of Clonmacnoise, was born of a distinguished Ossory family and (according to his *Life*) remained thirty years in Ireland before leaving to travel to Rome. Once there he was baptised and ordained by Pope Celestine and remained for another two decades. At the instigation of Saint Patrick (with whom he was not on very good terms) he then returned to Ireland, perhaps about 475, and settled near the well of Fuaran, in just about the centre of the country. Here he founded the monastery of Saighir (it is near Birr in the present Co. Offaly) which grew rapidly in size and fame and, in turn, gave rise to a number of daughter establishments. The cemetery at the monastery was considered to be of especial sanctity and became the burial-place of the royal house of Ossory. Ciaran's dates are difficult to determine and we can say little more than that he flourished in the late fifth-early sixth centuries. Despite the assertion of one of his early hagiographers, it is improbable that he lived to the age of three hundred and sixty. His feast day is 5 March.

The Latin text of both stories is to be found in Plummer, *Vitae Sanctorum Hiberniae* I: 219–20 (*cap.* v-vii).

COLUMBA OF IONA

Columba (or Columcille) was born about 520 in Ireland: in Gartan, in what is now Co. Donegal. He was trained as a monk from an early age and obviously demonstrated a genius for administration and organization as well as a true piety. He founded monasteries at Derry and Durrow—perhaps also at Kells—and in 563 sailed from Ireland with twelve companions to found the monastery of Iona. Here he was to remain for much of the rest of his life. His missionary endeavours (and successes) in Scotland have undoubtedly been much exaggerated, and although Columba was certainly important in this regard, he was not as important as many people think. He died in 597 (during the night of 8–9 June, if his biographer is correct) and was buried on Iona, but as a consequence of a number of Viking raids his relics were translated to Dunkeld in 849. His successor as abbot of Iona was his cousin and foster-son, Baithene, whom we shall meet in the second story.

The Latin texts of all four tales are to be found in *Adomnan's Life of Columba*, edited by A.O. and M.O. Anderson (London, 1961): 386–8 (II.27: the Loch Ness monster), 244–8 (I.19: the consequences of disobedience), 312–4 (I.48: hospitality), and 522–4 (III.23: the sorrow of Columba's horse).

Notes

The Loch Ness Monster

To the best of my knowledge, this is the earliest surviving record of a monster in the Loch. Whether it, or its descendants, are still there remains undetermined.

Lugne MacMin] Lugne went on to become prior of a monastery on the island of Elen (see *Adomnan's Life*, 364), but the 'island of Elen' has not been positively identified.

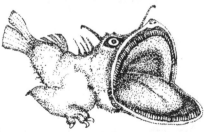

about fifteen feet] *unius contuli longitudo* 'the length of one pole'. The precise length of a pole at this time is unclear, but it was certainly much too close for comfort.

The Consequences of Disobedience

Berach] Nothing more is known of this monk.

Baithene] Baithene was a cousin of Columba and also, probably, his foster-son. He was at one time at the monastery on the island of Hinba, then prior of Mag-Lunge on Tiree, and after the death of Columba succeeded him as abbot of Iona. He died about the year 600.

to sail to the island of Tiree] Tiree lies about twenty miles northwest of Iona across what is now called the Passage of Skerryvore. The sea can be very rough there and it is not always pleasant sailing.

round by the little islands] presumably via Staffa, Lunga, and Fladda; then west to Coll and so down to Tiree. This is a much longer voyage than the direct northwest passage.

Hospitality

when the third hour before sunset has passed] literally, 'after the ninth hour of the day'.

CUTHBERT OF LINDISFARNE

Cuthbert was born in a fairly well-to-do family and became a monk at the abbey of Melrose in 651. About ten years later, after a brief spell at Ripon, he became prior of Melrose and over the next few years undertook a considerable number of missionary journeys around the north of England. After the Synod of Whitby in 663/4 he adopted Roman usages in the matter of the tonsure and the date of Easter, and was then

appointed prior of Lindisfarne, or Holy Island. In 676, however, he felt the need to live a more solitary life and left Lindisfarne for the inhospitable austerity of Inner Farne, a rocky
and wind-swept island about seven miles from Lindisfarne
and about a mile and a half from the English mainland. The
site of his hermitage is marked by the ruins of a fourteenth-
century chapel. Here he remained for eight years until 684,
when he was elected (much against his will) to the bishopric
of Hexham. In the next year, however, he was able to exchange
this see for that of Lindisfarne, and as bishop of Lindisfarne
he spent the remaining months of his life. He died on Inner
Farne on 20 March 687 (his feast is celebrated on this day) and
was initially buried in his episcopal church on Lindisfarne.
Almost two centuries later, when the island was pillaged by
the Danes, his coffin was unearthed and then began a series of
travels which ended only in 1104, when his relics found their
final resting-place in the great Norman cathedral at Durham. It
is appropriate that the Farne Islands are now a sanctuary for
the birds, seals, and other wild creatures which Cuthbert so
obviously appreciated and with which he enjoyed so intimate
a relationship.

   All five stories are taken from Bede's *Prose Life of Cuthbert* in B. Colgrave (ed./tr.), *Two Lives of Saint Cuthbert* (Cambridge, 1940). 'An equine provider' is chapter 5 (pages 168–70);
'What the brother saw' is chapter 10 (188–90); 'The
worker is worthy of her hire' is chapter 12 (194–6); 'The birds
and the barley' is chapter 19 (220–22); and 'The penitent
ravens' is chapter 20 (222–4).

Notes

An Equine Provider

Ingwald] nothing more is known of this monk.

our monastery at the mouth of the River Wear] the twin Benedictine monasteries of Wearmouth and Jarrow were founded in 674 and 682 respectively by Benedict Biscop. They became famous centres of learning and scholarship, and their great tradition was both maintained and magnified by Bede, who went to Wearmouth at the age of seven, transferred to Jarrow just after its foundation, and apart from visits to Lindisfarne and York, remained there as a monk for the rest of his life. In the second half of the ninth century the monasteries were destroyed by the Danes, but were restored by Aldwin in 1074 and soon established themselves once again as flourishing centres of religion and culture.

What the Brother Saw

the monastery of Melrose] the first monastery of Melrose was said to have been founded by Saint Aidan in the middle of the seventh century, but this foundation was destroyed in 839 by Kenneth, king of Scots. The second monastery was then established in the first half of the twelfth century by Cistercian monks from Rievaulx, and the magnificent ruins which can be seen today are those of the later Cistercian abbey, not those of Cuthbert's spiritual home.

The Birds and the Barley

The prototype of this tale (as Bede indicates) is a story told of Saint Antony by his biographer, Athanasius the Great. When Antony had settled on the 'inner mountain' of Mount Colzim (which is still called Deir Mar Antonios) he planted a small garden and irrigated it from a little spring. His own requirements were minimal, but because of his numerous visitors he planted some vegetables in the garden to provide for their needs. Unfortunately, the wild animals also found them tasty and would frequently come in and steal the crop. One day, then, Antony caught one of them and said: 'I do you no injury, so why do you hurt me? Go away, and in the Lord's

name don't come here again.' And, of course, they did not. The story occurs in chapter 50 of Athanasius's *Life of Antony*. Boniface, bishop of Ferentino, had the same problem with caterpillars (see Gregory the Great, *Dialogues* I,9), and similar stories, involving a variety of creatures, are to be found in the lives of a considerable number of saints. I tried Boniface's trick in my own garden, but it didn't work. I think I must have got the words wrong.

The Penitent Ravens

after the example of father Benedict] Bede is referring to the story of Benedict and the raven which we have translated above, s.v. Benedict of Nursia.

ELIJAH B. SOLOMON,
THE GAON OF WILNA

The Gaon was born in 1720 in a small town near Wilna (in Lithuania), but moved to the city with his family when very young. His father was a learned and respected scholar, and Elijah inherited all—and more—of his intelligence and character. His earliest important discourse was delivered in the main synagogue in Wilna at the age of seven. In his late teens and twenties he spent some years wandering amongst the Jewish communities of Poland and Germany, but returned to Wilna when he was twenty-eight and remained there for the rest of his life. His was an austere and ascetic piety, very different from the more emotional devotion of the *ḥasidim* of his day—he was, in fact, one of the most vigorous opponents of the hasidic movement—but his honesty, generosity, modesty, intelligence, learning, and authority were recognised by all the Jews of Lithuania and by a large proportion of those in eastern Europe generally. He died in 1797.

The Yiddish text of this anecdote is to be found in B. Yeushson (or A. H. Justman: both names are used), *Fun Unser Alt'n Oitzer: Volume I* (rpt. Tel Aviv, 1954) 10. The terms used are not easy to translate: what the cat contributes is *tseni'ūth* 'modesty, chastity, decency, discretion' (I conclude from this that the Gaon never had a cat); the leopard (or tiger) contributes *'azzūth*, which can mean impudence, arrogance, or impertinence, as well as courage and resolution. Much depends on the meaning—the sometimes altered meaning—of Hebrew loan-words in Yiddish.

FIRMINUS

Firminus, born about 516, was the third known bishop of Uzès. According to some sources, he was educated by his uncle, Roric, who was also bishop of Uzès and whom Firminus succeeded round about 538. Roric, however, is a very shadowy figure and it is much more likely that the second bishop of Uzès was a man named Probatius. Firminus was a friend and pupil of the renowned Caesarius of Arles and collaborated in writing the life of Caesarius between 542 and 549. He was a man of considerable influence in his time, attending a number of councils in Gaul in the late sixth century and being lauded by Arator in 544. He died about 553 and was succeeded, as Gerald tells us in this story, by his nephew—or probable nephew—Ferreolus. His feast day is October 11.

The Latin text of the story is to be found in the *Topographia Hibernica* of Gerald of Wales: *Giraldi Cambrensis: Topographia Hibernica et Expugnatio Hibernica*, ed. J. F. Dimock (Rolls Series 21/5; London, 1867) 115 (*Dist.* II *cap.* xxviii).

Notes

Uzès] Uzès is a small town in the south of France, about twelve miles north of present-day Nîmes. It was an episcopal see from the fifth century to 1790.

Saint Ferreolus] Ferreolus, as we have noted above, may very well have been the nephew of Firminus, though this is not absolutely certain. Whether nephew or not, he assuredly succeeded him as bishop of Uzès in about 553 and proved to be a competent and popular prelate. So popular was he, in fact, that the reigning king, Childebert I, became alarmed at the matter, saw him as a threat, and banished him to Paris for three years. After that period, however, Childebert's fears were put to rest and Ferreolus returned to his see where, in course of time, he died in 581. He is buried in the church of Saint Paul and is commemorated on 4 January. It is probable that he had a hand in the production of the so-called *Regula Ferreoli*, an important monastic code produced in Gaul in the late sixth century, but how much of a hand he had is not entirely clear.

FLORENTIUS

Florentius was a disciple of the saintly abbot Spes who had founded a monastery at Campli, some six miles from Nursia. For forty years Spes had been blind, but two weeks before his death his sight was miraculously restored. He spent the time preaching in all the monasteries in the neighbourhood, and at his death his soul was seen to fly up and away from his body in the form of a white dove. Florentius, his pupil, was the companion of Eutychius and the two of them lived as hermits in the Val Castoriana, a few miles from Nursia, in and around the year 487. Some time later, perhaps about 526, Eutychius was persuaded to become superior at Campli, but Florentius remained in his hermitage in the Val Castoriana until his death in June 548. Eutychius had died about two years earlier. Florentius was also responsible for dealing with an infestation of snakes in the area round his hermitage, and we have told the story above s.v. 'An Anonymous Monk of Fondi'.

The Latin text of the story is to be found in Gregory the Great, *Liber Dialogorum* III,15; PL 77: 249C–53A. For the times which I have translated as 'noon', 'three o'clock', and so on, the Latin text has 'the sixth hour', 'the ninth hour', etc.

FORTUNATUS

Fortunatus is known to us only from the first book of the *Dialogues* of Gregory the Great. We are told there that he was bishop of Todi in Umbria, and since one of the miracles he performed involved the Goths, and since the Goths left Italy in 553, his episcopate must have fallen sometime in the first half of the sixth century. Gregory tells us that he was noted for his power over evil spirits, but apart from attributing to him several miracles (mostly of the common or garden variety), he tells us very little else.

The Latin text of the present story is to be found in Gregory the Great, *Liber Dialogorum* I,10; PL 77: 204C–5A.

FRANCIS OF ASSISI

What shall we say of Francis? He was not a social reformer, not a pre-Marxian Marxist, not a sentimental and emotional lover of animals, not a streetperson, not a drop-out, not a sun-worshipper, not a sufi (at least, not a member of any specific Order), and probably not very much like his portrayal in the multitudinous books and movies which his remarkable life and personality have engendered. He was born in 1181 and, in his youth, was a true man-about-town. He fought for Assisi against Perugia, was captured, suffered a serious illness, and shortly after his release heard a voice in the derelict church of San Damiano telling him to repair God's house which, as he could see, was falling down. This was the beginning of the Franciscan Order and to follow its convoluted history is far beyond the scope of these brief notes. He and his disciples were true sons of Mother Church, devoted to the Pope and to doctrinal orthodoxy, and in their early days strove to live the gospel life with all its inevitable concomitant hardship. They begged for their food, they slept on the ground, they possessed as little as possible, they lived in huts which barely kept out the rain, their churches were small and unpretentious, and they preached—and their preaching was astonishingly successful. Francis himself was determined to preach to the Muslims as well as the Christians, and in 1219, accompanied by a dozen friars, made his way to Damietta. He rightly denounced the brutal, barbarian, crude, uncivilized, evil-living, savage, blood-stained, christian crusaders, and in some peculiar way did indeed make his way to the camp of the Sultan where he was very well received and listened to with the utmost courtesy. Why he ever came back to Christendom I cannot understand. Howbeit, back he came only to find that his Order had undergone major changes. It had grown too swiftly and was now too large, too disorganized, and too interested in ecclesiastical politics. The *Regula prima*, compiled in about 1210, was quite inadequate to keep control of an Order which now numbered more than five thousand. Francis therefore resigned his office as Minister-General (the year was 1220) and was succeeded by Elias of Cortona. He then drew up a second and more elaborate rule, and it was this which, with certain amendments and modifications, was given papal approval as the *Regula Bullata* in 1223. From his later years, when he no longer held any official position in the Order, date the Canticle of the Sun and the stigmata, and it was soon after receiving this last (mixed) blessing that he became ill and blind, and after suffering the usual painful and botched attempts at medicine and surgery, he died aged 45 in 1226. Two years later he was canonized and his feast day in 4 October.

Editions and versions of the *Fioretti*, the *Little Flowers* of Saint Francis, are legion, but for the Italian text of the three stories here translated I have relied upon Luciano Canonici's *I Fioretti di San Francesco* (Assisi, 1966) 70–72 (chapter 16: the sermon to the birds), 91–6 (chapter 21: the wolf of Gubbio), and 97–8 (chapter 22: Francis and the turtle-doves).

Notes

The Sermon to the Birds

Very similar—almost identical, in fact—to this famous story is the account in chapter 40 of the *Fioretti* of Saint Anthony of Padua preaching to the fishes. He was at Rimini at the time and was trying to preach the true faith to a great crowd of heretics who persistently refused to listen to him. Anthony therefore decided to preach to the fish instead, and a great crowd of them swam up to him, pushed their heads out of the water, and arranged themselves in proper order: the smallest ones were in front, the middling ones were in the middle, and at the back (where the water was deepest) were the largest ones. The sermon which followed is virtually identical to that which Francis preached to the birds, save that air becomes water and flying becomes swimming. The heretics were so impressed with this miracle that they changed their minds and decided to listen to Anthony after all (who wants to be upstaged by a fish?), and in this way they were converted and assured of Paradise.

Alviano] Alviano lies between Orte and Orvieto and the date would appear to be 1212–13. Something is obviously wrong here, however, for the Third Order was not established either in this place or at this time: it came into being in Florence in 1221. In some texts Alviano is replaced by Saburniano.

Cannara and Bevagna] Cannara is a large village located about thirteen miles south-east of Perugia, and Bevagna is a small town lying about three miles further on.

The Wolf of Gubbio

In its fully developed form, the story of the wolf of Gubbio dates from about a century after Francis's death; but whether it had its origins in the taming of a real animal or in the conversion of a robber of such ferocity that he was known as Il Lupo, 'The Wolf', is still debated. For our purposes it matters not at all: it is the story which is worth the telling.

Gubbio] Gubbio is a small town in Umbria, in central Italy, about nineteen miles northeast of Perugia. It still retains a decidedly medieval flavour and appearance.

GODRIC OF FINCHALE

The story of Godric of Finchale is quite astonishing and we are fortunate in having a very full and detailed life by Reginald of Durham. Godric was born shortly before 1070 at Walpole in Norfolk, became a peddler in his teens, and in 1089 made a pilgrimage to Rome. Thereafter he went to sea and became a successful merchant (his ventures may have been helped by a touch of piracy), and, it would seem, thoroughly enjoyed himself in the wicked ways of the world. He still, however, had a deep yearning for religion (the enjoyment of sin and a desire for sanctity may seem curious bedfellows, but the combination is a common one), and he undertook a number of pilgrimages to various holy places. Then, in about 1105, he sold all his possessions and tried to renounce the world and live as a hermit in the north of England, first near Carlisle, then near Durham. These first attempts at the eremitic life were not wholly successful, and Godric went on further pilgrimages. He worked for some time in a hospital in the Holy Land, returned to England, took up peddling again for a short time, but eventually made his way to Finchale, a most attractive site in a crook of the River Wear not far from the city of Durham. He was about forty at the time. Here he undertook a life of extraordinary asceticism and became known for his holiness, austerities, visions, and kindness both to animals and humans. He was also considered to have prophetic gifts, and towards the end of his life seems to have become a focal point for poltergeist phenomena. He became known throughout the Christian world (no less a person than Pope Alexander III wrote to him to ask for his prayers) and died, famed and acclaimed, on 21 May 1170. His feast is celebrated on that day.

Three of the stories presented here are taken from Reginald of Durham's life of Godric: *Libellus de Vita et Miraculis S. Godrici, Heremitae de Finchale, auctore Reginaldo Monacho Dunelmensis*, ed. J. Stevenson, Surtees Society 20 (London, 1847). 'The Greedy Deer' is to be found on pages 95–7 (*cap*. 39); 'Godric's care of the animals' on pages 98–9 (*cap*. 40); and 'The obedient cow' on pages 120–22 (*cap*. 51–52). The fourth story, 'God knows!' appears in the much shorter life by Geoffrey of Coldingham, *cap*. II, 20 (*Acta Sanctorum*, May 21, p.75). The Life of Godric is a splendid story and cries out for translation (though Reginald's Latin is not easy). There is, however, a wonderful short novel based on his life by Frederick Buechner, *Godric* (New York, 1980).

Notes

The Greedy Deer

Reginald tells a similar story about a hare: Godric had planted vegetables to feed the poor, but a little hare had discovered his plot and would come and feast on his plantings. Godric put up with this for some time, but then became annoyed and tracked down the little robber by following his paw-prints. As with the deer, he commanded it not to run away, and when he came up to it, he gave it a tap with his stick. But then he picked some of his vegetables, tied them on the hare's back in a bundle and sent it off into the woods. 'And don't come back!', said Godric, 'This food is meant for the poor.' Needless to say, the little hare obeyed his command. A cat, of course, would have paid the saint no attention whatever.

Godric's Care of the Animals

looked after the reptiles] Reginald tells us elsewhere that Godric enjoyed the company of snakes and had two of them as pets. They stayed with him for some time and would twine themselves round his legs. But eventually, when he found that their ophidian love distracted him from his prayers, he had to send them back into the woods, and he never saw them again.

God knows!

Ranulf, bishop of Durham] Ranulf Flambard, a devious and double-dealing ecclesiastic of the most questionable morals, was consecrated bishop of Durham on 5 June 1099 and died on 5 September 1128.

HELLE

Helle is known only from the account in the *Historia Monachorum in Aegypto*, and apart from saying that he was a fourth-century Egyptian ascetic, there is little that can usefully be added. His austerities and miracles were not especially unusual; but his treatment of the helpful crocodile cannot be said to be especially charitable. We might note that Pachomius is also said to have used crocodiles in this way: any time he needed to cross the Nile, one of them appeared to transport him. He, however, did not kill them off at the end of the trip. On the other hand, this convenient ferrying occurs only in the Greek lives of the saint (and their Latin translations). In the Bohairic life we have a different tale: Pachomius and another monk were soaking reeds in the river one day when a crocodile appeared. The other monk ran away, but Pachomius laughed: 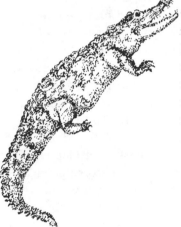'Do you think the wild beasts are their own masters?', he said. And when the crocodile came nearer, he flung a handful of water in its face, sent it packing, and told it never to come back again. This incident (of which a full translation may be read in the first volume of Armand Veilleux's admirable *Pachomian Koinonia* [CS 45; Kalamazoo, 1980] 43) may well be the basis for the later, rather more dramatic accounts.

The Greek texts of both the Helle stories are to be found in the *Historia Monachorum in Aegypto* XII: 5–9, ed. A. J. Festugière (Subsidia Hagiographica, no. 53; Brussels, 1971) 93–5.

ILLTUD

Illtud was one of the most important of the Welsh saints, but his life is difficult to reconstruct and is beset by chronological problems. He may have been born in Brittany (though this is not certain) and, according to tradition, as a young man he had no intention of pursuing either a monastic or a religious vocation. Instead, he crossed the Channel, married, and served under King Arthur, whence he gained one of his Welsh titles, *Illtud farchog* 'Illtud the Knight'. In course of time, however, he was converted from his worldly occupation and took the monastic habit, having callously driven his wife from both his bed and his house (one is reminded of the equally despicable treatment of his former mistress by Augustine of Hippo). She then became a nun, but later in her life evinced a desire to see Saint Illtud once again. She accordingly made her way to his monastery where she saw him working in the fields, dirty and lean. When she addressed him, he refused to answer and simply turned his back. As a consequence of this 'unseemly visit', says the *Vita*, she became blind, but Illtud at least had the courtesy to ask God to restore her sight. He did so; but ever afterwards her face was pale and spotty, and she never regained her former beauty. Sanctity, it seems, simply brings out the worst in some people. But to return to Illtud: after his conversion he settled at Hoddnant, near the River Severn, and from here he founded the monastery of Llantwit Major (*Llanilltud Fawr* in Welsh) which was to become one of the most important religious centres in Wales. Later still he returned for a time to his native Brittany in order to assist in relieving a famine (his own granaries at Llantwit were full to overflowing); came back once again to Wales; and then in advanced old age, returned to Brittany for the last time to die at Dol. Such, at least, is the tradition; whether it is correct is another matter. The chronological difficulties which we mentioned earlier prevent any accurate calculation of the dates of Illtud's birth and death, and we can say little more than that he died probably in the second or third decade of the sixth century. His feast day is 6 November. I do not think he was a particularly nice person.

The Latin text of the story is to be found in Wade-Evans, *Vitae Sanctorum Britanniae et Genealogiae* (see above s.v. Brynach), 212–4. In the last few sentences the writer lapses into verse.

Notes

the disciple Samson] this is the Samson who was later
to become bishop of Dol in Brittany, and who was one of the
most important missionaries of sixth-century Britain. He was
educated by Illtud at Llantwit Major and there ordained bishop
and priest. Later he visited Caldey Island, Ireland, Cornwall,
the Scilly Isles (probably), Normandy (where he founded a
monastery at Pental), and Brittany. He died in 565 and is commemorated on 28 July.

by rendering them incapable of flight] the Latin text
says simply *sine volatibus* 'without flying'.

JEROME

The formidable Jerome was born at Strido, near
Aquileia, about 341 and, in due course, was given a sound and
thorough education first by his father and then by the famous
grammarian Donatus. In his mid-twenties he travelled extensively in France and Italy, and then, together with some friends
in Aquileia, decided to became a monk. Shortly thereafter, as
a result of some quarrel (Jerome was not known for his equa-
nimity), he left for Palestine and lived the hermit life in the
Syrian desert. It was here that he mastered Hebrew. He was ordained priest in Antioch, studied for some time in Constantinople under no less a figure than Gregory of Nazianzus, and
then returned to Rome in 382. In Rome, as assistant to Pope
Damasus, he began the immense task of producing a standard
Latin translation of the Bible, the version which we know as
the Vulgate; but in 385, after only three years, he left the city
(his vicious temper and his sarcastic tongue seem once again
to have got him into trouble) and set off for Bethlehem. Here
he was to spend the rest of his life. It was in his monastery

at Bethlehem that he met the lion (the story shows the better side of his somewhat aggressive character), and it was here that he died in 420. His feast-day is 30 September. A similar—indeed, almost identical—story of a donkey and a lion appears in the *Spiritual Meadow* of John Moschus (chapter 107), there attributed not to Jerome but to Abba Gerasimus. A complete translation may be found in Helen Waddell's *Beasts and Saints* (London, 1934) 25–9.

The Latin text of the story is to be found at the end of the *Vita Sancti Hieronymi* often attributed (incorrectly) to Sebastian of Monte Cassino, PL 22: 210–13.

Notes

a gallon and a half of oil] lit. 'one *hin* of oil': the *hin*, a Hebrew measure for liquids, seems to have been about six litres.

JESUS OF NAZARETH

The source of these two stories is the apocryphal work sometimes called the Gospel of Pseudo-Matthew, but more commonly the *Liber de ortu beatae Mariae et infantia Salvatoris* (Book of the Birth of Blessed Mary and the Infancy of the Saviour) supposedly written by Matthew and translated into Latin by Jerome. It is, in fact, a Western production dating from the sixth century and its main sources are the *Protevangelium Jacobi*, one of the versions of the Infancy Gospel of Pseudo-Thomas, and certain other miscellaneous records which remain unidentified. The stories translated here derive from this third group of material and do not appear in either Pseudo-Thomas or the *Protevangelium*. It need hardly be added that Matthew did not write the gospel; Jerome did not translate it (the prefatory letter is spurious); and its historical value is minimal. But I happen to like the two tales here presented, and, as the Italians say, *se non é vero, é ben trovato*.

The Latin text of both stories may be found in A. de Santos Otero, *Los Evangelios Apócrifos* (Biblioteca de Autores Cristianos 148; Madrid, 1963 [second edition]) 216–8 (*cap.* xviii-xix [The Procession of the Animals]) and 234–6 (*cap.* xxxv-xxxvi [The Superiority of Animals]).

Notes

The Superiority of Animals

a road which leaves Jericho and leads to the River Jordan] from Jericho to Jordan in an easterly walk of about ten miles.

where the Ark of the Covenant is said to have rested] see Joshua 4: 1–14.

where a lioness was rearing her cubs] there are now no lions in Israel, but there certainly were when Jesus was eight years old. The records of Greek travellers tell us that a few could still be found as late as the twelfth century.

the water of the Jordan was divided to the right hand and the left] just as it had been for Joshua and, later, for Elijah (see 2 Kings 2:8).

JOHN THE EVANGELIST

The text from which this curious tale is taken is a Coptic apocryphon entitled *The Mysteries of John the Apostle and*

Holy Virgin. It begins, as we have said, with Christ returning
to the Mount of Olives after his resurrection and granting John
the privilege of visiting heaven and satisfying his curiosity on
a number of important questions. What, for example, is the
reason for famine and drought? How did creation take place?
Where did wheat come from? What will happen at the end
of time? How tall was Adam in Eden? (The answer, for those
who are curious, is that he was about twenty feet high, ten
feet wide, and his neck was five feet long). Is the length of a
person's life pre-ordained? And so on. It is an intriguing text
and is available only in an unsatisfactory edition with a barely
adequate English translation in E. A. Wallis Budge, *Coptic Apoc-
rypha in the Dialect of Upper Egypt* (*Coptic Texts*, Vol. III; London,
1913). The Coptic text of the section here translated appears on
page 71.

Notes

       outside the veil] behind the veil is the throne of God
and God himself.
       when the twelfth cherub has ended, the twelfth hour
has ended] Budge's text actually says 'when the twelfth hour
has ended, the twelfth hour has ended,' and obviously requires
emendation.

JOHN I

       John I, a friend of Boethius, was old and infirm when
he was elevated to the papacy on 13 August 523, and immediately after his election he became involved with the unfortunate anti-Arian measures of the eastern emperor Justin I.

The latter hated heresy with a passion, but his attacks on Arianism were also attacks on the Goths who, for the most part, found the Arian approach to the Trinity more to their liking. Theodoric, the ruler of Italy at the time, was himself a Goth (and an Arian) and was understandably annoyed—as well as a little nervous—when Justin's persecution began. He therefore contacted John and ordered him to take a delegation to Constantinople, talk to Justin, and rectify the matter. If he did not (said Theodoric) things might get nasty for the Catholics in Italy. John left for the east in 526, and it was on his journey that the events narrated in this story took place. His embassy to Constantinople was not entirely successful—he could not get Justin to agree that Arians should be allowed total freedom of worship—and when he returned to Italy and told Theodoric of this, the latter was infuriated and ordered the pope to stay in Ravenna until he decided what to do with him. As it happened, he was forestalled by death: John was already old and sick, and the strain of his travels, together with his justified anxiety about what Theodoric was going to do, was just too much for him, and he died on 18 May 526. He was later canonized and his feast is commemorated on the day of his decease.

The Latin text of the tale is to be found in Gregory the Great, *Liber Dialogorum* III, 2; PL 77: 221B–4A.

Notes

Justin] Justin I, mentioned above, who was the eastern emperor from 518 to 527. He is here called *senior princeps*. His hatred of heresy (as he defined it) and his rabid Chalcedonianism led to a number of unfortunate consequences for the east as well as the west.

JUDAH THE PRINCE

Rabbi Judah the Prince, or Judah ha-Nasi (the title indicates the president of the Great Sanhedrin which, at this time, was located in Galilee) was the son of Rabbi Simeon ben Gamaliel and was born in 135. He was on friendly terms with the Roman authorities, even with one of the Roman emperors (though which one is not entirely clear: it may have been Marcus Aurelius), and was thereby able to mitigate—and to mitigate very considerably—the series of vicious persecutions which had followed the fall of Jerusalem and the crushing of the Second Jewish Revolt in the year of his birth. For some fifty years Rabbi Judah managed to secure for the Jews some measure of peace and stability, and it was during these years that he and his colleagues were to compile that important and authoritative digest of the Oral Torah which is Rabbi Judah's true monument: the Mishnah. So great was his fame in Judaism, and so esteemed was his learning, that in rabbinic texts he is simply known as 'Rabbi', the Teacher; and when he died in 217, it was said that the glory had departed from Israel.

We may compare with this anecdote a tale told of Rūmī by Aflākī in his *Manāqib al-'ārifīn* (see below s.v. Rūmī) I: 174–5 (section 3/89): one day, we are told, Rūmī was on his way to visit his father's tomb when a cow, which, like the calf in Sepphoris, was being taken to slaughter, broke away from its captors and fled through the streets. Everyone started to chase it but none could catch it; and eventually, in its mad flight, the animal encountered Rūmī. It immediately stopped running, came up to our Master, and seemed to ask for protection. Rūmī stroked and patted it. When the butchers arrived in hot pursuit, they saw Rūmī with the animal and naturally asked for it to be returned. Rūmī refused. 'This beast is not to be killed,' he said; 'set her free.' And such was his authority that the butchers obeyed him, and the cow made her way back to the pastures.

Just then Rūmī's dis-
ciples came on the scene and
the Master said to them: 'An
animal destined for death fled
and came to us, but God (may
He be magnified and exalted!)
delivered her from death. So
when human beings turn to
God with all their heart and
soul, will He not deliver them
from the fires of Hell and bring them to Paradise? Of course
He will!' And it was said that the cow which Rūmī had saved
was never seen again in the meadows of Konya.

The story of R. Judah translated here is a composite
version: it is based on the Aramaic text in *The Babylonian Talmud, Seder Nezikin, Baba Mezia, Volume II* (New York, 1959) 85a,
supplemented with material from the Hebrew version of the
story in *Midrash Rabbah* (the Wilna edition of 1878, edited by B.
Romm), Bereshith Rabbah, Noah, parashah 33.3 (Genesis page
136 col. 2 in Romm's edition). The last sentence is taken from a
later rabbinic commentary.

Notes

Sepphoris] Sepphoris is the modern Saffurye, lying in
the hills of lower Galilee about four miles north of Nazareth. It
was the capital of the territory of Herod Antipas and a beautiful city in its day.

weasels] *karkūshtā* in Aramaic. The Hebrew version
simply talks about reptiles (*sheretz*), but the point of the story
is that whatever they were, they were ritually unclean, and
no orthodox Jew would want to have them around. But Rabbi
Judah—the greatest authority on religious Law in the Jewish
world of his day, the light of Israel, the Teacher *par excellence*—
says 'Let them be'.

KEVIN

The name Kevin, commonly given to this saint, is an attempt at reproducing the pronunciation of his actual Irish name, Caoimhghin (and variants), which in turn appears in the Latin life as Coemgen. Irish spelling, prior to the reforms of 1948, is even worse than English. He was born of a noble Leinster family and from an early age was trained and educated for the monastic life. After his ordination, he moved to Glendalough (in what in now Co. Wicklow) and settled there as a hermit, possibly occupying the early rock-tomb which is still to be seen there and which is known as 'Saint Kevin's Bed'. It is an amazingly beautiful and romantic spot. His sanctity immediately attracted disciples, and in the course of time so many of them flocked to the area that the monastic buildings at the Upper Lake, where Kevin had originally settled, proved too small to house them. After the saint's death, therefore, the monastery was moved to the Lower Lake where more land was available. Glendalough was to become one of the most important religious centres in Ireland (seven pilgrimages to Glendalough were the equivalent of one pilgrimage to Rome), and it was to magnify its claims and increase its fame that the *Vitae* of Kevin, both in Latin and Irish, were composed. All of them date from at least four centuries after his death (which occurred probably about 620) and none of them is a reliable source of biographical information. His feast day is 3 June.

The Latin texts of the stories of 'Saint Kevin at Prayer' and 'The Greedy Ravens' may be found in Plummer, *Vitae Sanctorum Hiberniae* I: 243–4 (*cap.* xix) and 250–51 (*cap.* xxxi-xxxii); the tale of Saint Kevin and the blackbird is in Gerald of Wales, *Topographia Hibernica* (see above s.v. Firminus) Dist. II, *cap.* xxviii (p. 116 of Dimock's edition).

Notes

Saint Kevin and the Blackbird

A similar story is told of Saint Malo by his biographer, Sigebert of Gembloux. One day, when the saint was working in the fields, he took off his cloak and folded it up on the ground. When he came to put it on again, he found that a wren had used it for her nest and laid her eggs on it. Naturally, he left it there until the eggs hatched and the chicks left. But for the whole period of the incubation, says Sigebert, no rain fell on the cloak or the nest. And there are many other examples of this sort of courtesy. Those who have cats will be well aware of the agonies suffered in cramped and constricted limbs as a consequence of the creatures deigning to take their repose on one's lap or one's knees. One does not even *think* of moving.

until the chicks were fully hatched] for those interested, the incubation period for the eggs of the blackbird is between eleven and seventeen days (it would have been of assistance to the mother if Saint Kevin had a warm hand), but the fledglings would require about another two weeks before they could leave the nest.

LIBERTINUS

Libertinus became prior of the monastery of Saint Magnus at Fondi after the death of Honoratus (some comments on Honoratus and Fondi will be found above s.v. 'An Anonymous Monk of Fondi'), but apart from the information provided by Gregory the Great in the first book of his *Dialogues*, nothing is known of him. Even Gregory's account is limited, and records only a few miracles and a story illustrating Libertinus's humility.

The Latin text of the tale is to be found in Gregory the Great, *Liber Dialogorum* I,2; PL 77: 157A–60A.

Notes

Totila, king of the Goths] Totila, a youthful but brilliant commander, became king of the Goths in 541, and set about reconquering the whole of Italy which had recently been 'liberated' by the Byzantines. Naples fell in 543, and Rome in 546; and apart from a few minor setbacks, his swift conquests continued unabated. The eastern emperor Justinian finally roused himself to deal with the situation and, with a huge army, set forth to meet Totila at Taginae in the early summer of 552. In this dramatic battle, the Goths were defeated; Totila was slain; and the Gothic state disappeared from history.

Samnium] one of the principal regions of Central Italy, dominated by the Matese mountains.

the river Volturno] the Volturno is the principal river of southern Italy. It rises in the Apennines, flows through Campania past Capua, and debouches into the Mediterranean about twenty-two miles northwest of Naples.

all the soldiers regained control of their own mounts] lit. 'all were recovered by each'.

MACARIUS

There are two famous Macarii—Macarius the Great and
Macarius of Alexandria—and they are frequently confused.
In the *Lausiac History*, for example, the story of the grateful
hyena is attributed to Macarius of Alexandria, but in the *Historia Monachorum in Aegypto* to Macarius the Great. We cannot
be sure, therefore, which Macarius did what.

Macarius the Great or Macarius of Egypt or Macarius
the Elder was born about the year 300 in a village in Upper
Egypt. When he was thirty he joined a group of monks in the
desert of Scetis and soon became famous for his asceticism and
miracles. By the age of forty he was renowned for his gifts
of healing and for his power to forecast the future. It seems
that he was ordained a priest, perhaps about 340, but little is
known of the details of his life. The career of a desert-dwelling
ascetic is, after all, hardly the material for a Harlequin Romance. He died about 390, and the small community which he
established at Scetis was the nucleus for the great monastery of
Saint Macarius which is still one of the most important monastic centres in Egypt. The relics of the saint are preserved in
the church. The well-known (and extraordinarily interesting)
homilies traditionally attributed to Macarius are certainly not
by him, and it is doubtful whether they were ever produced in
Egypt at all.

Macarius of Alexandria was a contemporary of Macarius the Great: he was probably born a little earlier and died a
little later than his more famous namesake. He settled in the
desert of Cellia (where Palladius met him) about 335, but few
of his sayings have been preserved, and the single sermon and
two monastic rules attributed to him are not authentic.

The Greek text of 'The Price of a Mosquito' is to be
found in C. Butler (ed.), *The Lausiac History of Palladius: Volume II* (Cambridge, 1904; rpt. Hildesheim, 1967) 48–9 (chapter
XVIII); that of 'Gratitude' is a composite text: it is based on
the account in the *Historia Monachorum in Aegypto* XXI: 15–16

(page 127 of Festugière's edition: see above s.v. Helle), but there are two minor additions from the version in chapter XVIII of the *Lausiac History* (page 57 of Butler's edition).

Notes

Gratitude

The Coptic version of this story is considerably longer, and at the end, when the hyena brings Macarius the sheepskin, he refuses to take it. 'Where did you get this?', he says. 'Have you killed a sheep?' And she obviously had. 'Well (says Macarius) I'll accept it only on one condition: in future you mustn't kill things, and you can eat them only if they're already dead. But if it should happen that you're hungry and can't find anything, then come here to me and I'll feed you.'

And so, now and again, when food was scarce, she would come to the holy old man and he would give her a loaf of bread from his supply. And as for the sheep-skin: Macarius used it to sleep on until he died. This skin is still pointed out today] according-ing to Palladius, it was in the possession of Melania the Elder, a rich and saintly woman who was born in Spain, but then moved to Rome where she married. After the death of her husband when she was twenty-two, she devoted herself to charity and good works and travelled extensively. Indeed, she seems to have collected holy men and ascetics like some people collect stamps. In due course she built a monastery on the Mount of Olives in Jerusalem and lived there for nearly thirty years.

In 397 she returned to Italy, but in 408, when the country was being threatened by the Goths, she fled to Jerusalem and died there two years later. The well-known *Life of Saint Melania* is not her life, but that of her equally saintly grand-daughter, Melania the Younger. It seems that sanctity ran in the family.

MAEDOC OF FERNS

Maedoc of Ferns is the same person as Aidan of Ferns: what has happened is that the original Irish name, Aedh, has been enlarged by a prefix, *mo* (which is a term of endearment) and a suffix, *oc* (which is a diminutive), to form Mo-aedh-oc or Maedoc, which we might translate literally as 'dear little Aedh'. He was born in Connacht (his mother was of royal stock), but although he began his education in Leinster, he soon moved to Wales and was trained under Saint David himself at his school in Dyfed. At this time, however, Christianity in Ireland was in a dangerous and unstable condition, for the initial impetus given to it by Patrick and his colleagues had died down and the old paganism was once again rearing its head. Aidan/Maedoc therefore returned to Ireland to help salvage the faith and founded monastic centres at Rossinver, Drumlane, and (most importantly) at Ferns in what is now Co. Wexford. He was a great friend of Molua of Clonfert (who also appears in this anthology) and both saints appear to have had a particular liking for wolves. On one occasion, for example, the wolves around Ferns carried off the calf of one of Maedoc's cows and the monastery cook came to tell the saint that the mother was mooing and obviously greatly distressed. Maedoc then made the sign of the cross over the cook and told him to go and offer his own head to the cow. When he did so, the cow licked it, and loved him like her own calf. A very odd story. Maedoc died about 626 and is commemorated on 31 January. Despite the appearance in older hagiographical materials of two Saint Maedocs of Ferns—Maedoc the Elder and Maedoc the Younger, both commemorated on the same day—there was almost certainly only one of him.

The Latin text of the story is to be found in Plummer, *Vitae Sanctorum Hiberniae* II: 143 (*cap.* vii).

Notes

his wax writing-tablet] the Latin text certainly says *ceraculum*, but it is by no means clear that this is what is intended. Certain manuscripts read *oraculum*, which is some object associated with praying, and the Irish lives prefer to think in terms of a rosary (*paidrin* in Irish). Since *ceraculum* may well represent such words as *cerculum* or *circulum*, the term could also refer to a girdle or even a ring. The precise nature of the object which Maedoc placed on the antlers of the fortunate stag therefore remains in some doubt.

MOLING

Moling or Mullins came from Leinster (his father claimed descent from the first Christian king of the area) and, like so many saints, is said to have embraced the religious life at an early age. In due course he founded his monastery of St Mullins on the bank of the river Barrow in what is now Co. Carlow. Later still, he was appointed bishop of Ferns in Co. Wexford, but in his old age he retired back to the monastery which he had founded and died there about 696. There is a holy well and a church dedicated to the saint in South Wales, but whether he himself ever left Ireland is uncertain and, perhaps, unlikely. His feast day is 17 June.

The Latin text of all five stories is to be found in Plummer, *Vitae Sanctorum Hiberniae* II: 199–203 (*cap.* xxi-xxiv, xxvii).

Notes

The Cat, the Wren, and the Fly

the druid of birds] i.e. a wren. The name 'the druid of birds' reflects a fanciful etymology of the wren's Irish name.

Bibliophagy

stole a book... intending to eat it] one must remember that books  at this time were written on vellum, which is simply scraped and prepared animal skin. They were therefore perfectly edible, though possibly somewhat tasteless. For Moling's fox, a good book would be the equivalent of a raw-hide bone.

The Last Visit of the Foxes

city of Ferns] in these Irish texts, 'city' (*civitas*) can mean city or monastery (or both) depending on the context.

In a little while I shall leave this city and go back to my own place] the 'city' is both the monastery of which he was abbot and the city of which he was bishop; the 'place' (*locus*) is likewise the monastery/*locus* of St Mullins which he founded and the true 'place' or *locus* of any monk: heaven.

MOLUA

According to tradition, Molua or Lua or Lugaigh (or a number of other spellings) was educated at Clonard by the venerable Saint Finian, abbot of Clonard, who was indeed renowned as a teacher and is said to have trained more than three thousand disciples. He later moved to the abbey of Bangor (which was to become the largest monastery in Ireland) where he became a monk and a priest under the tutelage of the equally famous Saint Comgall (who also trained Columbanus). Molua himself then went on to found Clonfert-molua (or Clonfert-mulloe), which is now called Kyle and lies in the Slievebloom Mountains between Offaly and Leix. He also founded a considerable number of smaller *loca* (more than a hundred, according to tradition), wrote for them a severe Rule (all Celtic Rules were severe), and went to Rome to have the Rule approved by Gregory the Great. Whether he was also the founder of Killaloe in Co. Clare in unclear: Molua was not an especially uncommon name, and it is possible that the Molua of Killaloe was a quite different person. Molua died about 608 and his feast day is 4 August.

The Latin text of the story is to be found in Plummer, *Vitae Sanctorum Hiberniae* II: 217–8 (*cap.* xxxiii).

MOSHE LEIB OF SASOV

Rabbi Moshe Yehudah Leib of Sasov (a town in the Ukraine, about five miles northeast of Zolochev), usually referred to as the Sassover, was a famous hasidic teacher and the disciple of an even more famous teacher, Rabbi Schmelke of Nikolsburg, who died in 1778. Rabbi Schmelke was the brother of Rabbi Pinchas of Frankfurt, whom we shall meet a little later on. The Sassover followed his teacher from town to town in his native Poland until he was finally appointed rabbi of Sasov. He was known for his great compassion, and it was said of him that whenever he saw anyone suffering or in pain, he took their sufferings upon himself to such an extent that they actually became his own. He would visit the sick in Sasov, especially the children, and is reported to have said: 'Anyone who is unwilling to suck the pus from the sores of a plague-stricken child has not climbed halfway up the mountain of love for his fellow human beings.' True love, said the Sassover, is to know what people need and to bear the burden of their sufferings. He died in 1807.

The German text of this story is to be found in Chajim Bloch, *Die Gemeinde der Chassidim: Ihr Werden und ihre Lehre, ihr Leben und ihr Treiben* (Berlin/Vienna, 1920) 188.

MOSES

Immediately before this story in the *Midrash Rabbah* we find a similar tale told of King David. Why was he chosen to rule over Israel? Because he was tried by God. How was he tried? By tending flocks. The Holy One, blessed be He, found that David was a good shepherd because he took the greatest care as to how he let the sheep out to pasture. First he would release the smallest ones so that they could graze on the tenderest grass; then he would let out the mature adults so that they could feed on the ordinary grass; and finally he would release the strongest and healthiest animals who could eat the tough shoots of the grass which were left over. Whereupon the Holy One, blessed be He, said: 'Since you know how to look after sheep and to give to each one the care that it needs, you

shall come and tend my people'; as it is written: 'From tending the ewes that had young He brought him to be shepherd over Jacob his people' (Ps 78:71).

That God is concerned about animals is made clear, again in *Midrash Rabbah*, by Rabbi Judah ben Pazzi: why is an infant not circumcised until the eighth day, asks the rabbi? Because God is merciful to the child and wants to delay the rite so as to give him time to develop his strength. And just as God is merciful to human beings, so he is merciful to cattle. How do we know? Because it says in Leviticus 22:27 that an animal may be accepted as an offering only from the eighth day, and in Leviticus 22:28 that you shall not kill both the animal and its young on the same day. And just as God is merciful to cattle, so he is merciful to birds. How do we know? Because it says in Deuteronomy 22:6 that if you are out walking and come across a bird's nest, you shall not take the mother with the chicks (*Debarim Rabbah*, Ki thetze, parashah 6.1).

The Hebrew text of the story of Moses is to be found in *Midrash Rabbah*, ed. B. Romm (Wilna, 1878), Shemoth, parashah 2.2 (Exodus page 17 col. 2 in Romm's edition). I have included one or two explanatory additions.

Notes

a place where leek-plants were growing] I have followed Romm's text here, but 'leek-plants' is not the only reading of the word in question (*chasith*), and there are a number of suggestions as to where the young kid got to: some authorities suggest a shaded place, some a ravine, some a wadi. The important point is, of course, the presence of water, and the leek-plant grows near marshy ground.

picked up the kid, put it on his shoulder] *lit.* 'caused it to ride on his shoulder'.

MUḤAMMAD

Muḥammad's love of cats is well known. Perhaps the most famous story is that which tells how his favourite cat, Mu'ezza ('the crier' or 'she who miaows people to prayer'), settled herself on the sleeve of the Messenger's robe in a place which, in typical feline fashion, was most convenient for her and most inconvenient for everybody else. But when it was time for prayer, Muḥammad (on whom be peace!) refused to wake the sleeping animal and instead cut off the sleeve of his garment so that she would not be disturbed. On another occasion, one of the Messenger's cats produced kittens on his robe; and according to another tradition, he promised a woman the pains of Hell because she had mistreated a cat. On the other hand, a woman who had brought water to a dog who was dying of thirst (and dogs are ritually unclean animals for Muslims) was guaranteed Paradise.

The tale translated here contains the ultimate *ḥadīth*, or prophetic tradition, for the cat-lover: 'love of cats is part of faith'. I had always believed this to be so, but was never more delighted when I discovered that it had prophetic authority. A variant of the story tells us that when the Messenger stroked the cat, his fingers left marks on her forehead; as a consequence of this, every kitten now born has some black stripes over the eyes. They are there on black cats, too, but you can't see them because of the colour. Abū Hureira's cat, incidentally, was promised Paradise because of her action.

The Persian text of the story (the *ḥadīth* is in Arabic) is to be found in Aflākī's *Manāqib al-'ārifīn* (for full bibliographical details, see under Rūmī, below), I: 477–478 (section 3/452).

Notes

Jand and Khojand] Jand was a small settlement near Khoresm on the Khiva oasis in what is now northwest Uzbekistan, and Khojand (or Khodzhent) was a large and ancient city on the Syr Darga near its exit from the Fergana valley. It is now in Tadzhikistan and in 1936 its name was changed to Leninabad. Whether the students we are talking about actually came from these places is another matter.

our Master Jalāl-ud-Dīn Rūmī] for an account of Rūmī, see below s.v. Rūmī.

the Chosen of God, Muḥammad] the text simply gives the name Muṣṭafa. It means 'the chosen', and is a name frequently used for Muḥammad in Persian literature.

the *miḥrāb* of the mosque at Qubā'] the *miḥrāb* is the large niche or indentation in the wall of a mosque which indicates the direction of Mecca. It therefore shows the way Muslims must face when at prayer. The mosque at Qubā' is one of the earliest mosques of Islam and is situated on high ground at the southern edge of the Medinan oasis. It was here that Muḥammad arrived on 24 September, 622 during the *hijrah*, or 'emigration', from Mecca, and here that he stayed for two or three days before moving a mile or so further north to what was to become his dwelling place in Medina, and, ultimately, the Prophet's Mosque. Some authorities say that the Qubā' mosque was founded by the Messenger; others that there was already a mosque at Qubā' at the time the Messenger arrived.

Abū Hureira] the name or, more accurately, nickname (*kunya*) Abū Hureira means 'father of the little cat', and was bestowed on this companion of the Prophet because of his obvious affection for the animals. He came to Medina in 629, seven years after the *hijrah*, and lived with Muḥammad until the latter's death. He was the source of a great many prophetic traditions (many are far from reliable), and died in his seventy-eighth year sometime between 676 and 678.

NANNAN

Of all the saints here represented, none is more obscure than Nannan. The name does not appear in any of the Irish martyrologies (though Ninians are far from uncommon) and I have no idea precisely which saint Gerald of Wales had in mind when he told this remarkable story. Nannan's fleas are his sole claim to fame and I can certainly testify to the fact that a young cat of my acquaintance, named for obvious reasons Winnie la Puce, was thoroughly cleansed of her uninvited guests by being deloused and having her name changed to Nannana.

The Latin text of the story is to be found in Gerald of Wales, *Topographia Hibernica* (see above, s.v. Firminus) *Dist.* II *cap.* xxxi (p. 119 of Dimock's edition).

NŪRĪ

Abū'l-Ḥusayn Aḥmad ibn Muḥammad an-Nūrī was a native of Baghdad and a friend of Junayd, one of the greatest and most revered of the Sufis. More than a century before his time, the remarkable woman mystic, Rābi'a al-'Adawiyya, had taught the importance of a pure and unadulterated love for God (what Saint Bernard was later to call 'chaste love', *amor castus*), a love which existed simply for God's sake and asked for nothing in return. 'O God,' she prayed, 'if I worship you through fear of Hell, burn me in Hell; and if I worship you in hope of Paradise, exclude me from Paradise. But if I worship you for your own sake, then do not grudge me your eternal beauty.' It is this concept of pure and disinterested love—a love which God does not need and for which he offers no reward—which is taken up by Nūrī and which forms the focal point of his spirituality. The manner of his death was somewhat strange, though not, perhaps, unfitting. One day he heard a blind man crying 'God! God!', and the cry so affected him that he became rapt in ecstasy. In this state he rushed into some nearby reed-beds where the reeds had just been cut, and the sharp stumps and edges pierced his feet and sliced into his sides to such a degree that the blood poured forth. But every drop that fell to the ground formed the words 'God! God!' When they brought him back home, it was clear that he was dying from loss of blood, and those attending him said to him, 'Say: There is no god but God.' In this way he would leave this life with the confession of faith on his lips and so enter Paradise. 'I'm on my way there,' said Nūrī, and died. The year was 908.

The Persian text of the story is to be found in Farīd-uddīn 'Attār, ed. R. A. Nicholson, *The Tadhkiratu'l-Awliya of Muḥammad ibn Ibrāhīm Farīdu'd-Dīn 'Aṭṭār* (London, 1907) II: 52 lines 9–11. For the manner of his death, see *ibid.*, II: 55 lines 5–12.

Notes

Shiblī] Abū Bakr ibn Jaḥdar ash-Shiblī was a high government official (he was Governor of Demavend) before his conversion to Sufism. After his conversion, he was (like Nūrī) associated with Junayd, but the sober spirituality of the latter is very different from the eccentric and ecstatic behaviour of the former. It seems probable, in fact, that Shiblī was actually a manic-depressive, and he was certainly committed for a time to an asylum. Nevertheless, his total and one-pointed love for God was never in doubt, and he demonstrated it in both words and actions. One day, for example, his friends saw him running along carrying flaming coals, and when they asked him where he was going he told them that he was going to set fire to the Kaaba in Mecca so that in future people would concern themselves only with God, the Lord of the Kaaba. On another occasion, they saw him carrying a piece of wood burning at both ends. 'What are you going to do?' they asked. 'I shall set Hell on fire with one end,' he replied, 'and Paradise on fire with the other. Then people will care only about God.' Shibli died in 945 aged 86 or 87.

OWAIN AP CARADOG AP IESTYN

We have moved here into the realm of medieval Welsh history and Owain, one of the four sons of Caradog ap Iestyn, was no saint. Caradog had married Gwladus, daughter of Gruffydd, the eldest son of the Lord Rhys (one of the greatest of the Welsh princes), and was lord of Rhwng Nedd ac Afan, holding the district and castle of Aberafan in South Wales. His father, Iestyn, is a shadowy figure who lost a kingdom, but gained a holy death in advanced old age in the priory of Llangenydd. The four unruly sons of Caradog were continually  at each others' throats, and Owain, the owner of the remarkable greyhound, was eventually murdered by his brother Cadwallon (who, in turn, came to a bad end). The events narrated by Gerald of Wales probably took place shortly before 1175.

After telling the story of the dog and the soldier, Gerald goes on to inform us that dogs trust their noses rather than their eyes, and that whereas the tongue of a wolf can cause death, that of a dog has healing powers. That is why a dog always licks itself if it has been injured. And if it cannot reach the site of the injury with its tongue, says our author, it will lick one of its hind feet and use that to transfer the healing saliva to the appropriate place. Gerald of Wales was always credulous.

The Latin text of the story is to be found in the *Itinerarium Kambriae* I, vii (J. F. Dimock [ed.], *Giraldi Cambrensis Opera* (Rolls Series 21/6; London, 1868) VI: 69–71).

Notes

The *De animantium naturis* of Suetonius is otherwise unknown; in Ambrose's *Hexameron*, the story is to be found in VI, 4, 24. Gerald, however, has amended and expanded Ambrose's text.

PAUL THE GREEK

So far as I am aware, nothing is known of Paul save that he was apparently Greek, that he lived for some time in a cave in the Holy Land, and that he flourished probably in the second half of the sixth century. This is little enough to go on, but more than we know of some of these obscure ascetics. Indeed, in some cases we know less than nothing (i.e. what we do know is wrong).

Notes

Calamon] Calamon or Kalamon was a lavra built between 452 and 470 just over a mile from the banks of the Jordan. It was one of a group of five communities lying midway between Jericho and the Dead Sea (one of the others—the lavra of abba Peter—is mentioned in the second story in this collection). The name means 'the monastery of the reeds', and refers to the tall reeds which grow on the banks of a small stream which flows very close to the monastery and which joins the Jordan a short distance away.

PINCHAS HURWITZ OF FRANKFURT

Rabbi Pinchas Hurwitz (or Phineas Horowitz) was born in Lithuania in 1740 and, as this tale indicates, spent some time as rabbi in Lakhovitch. In 1771, however, he was elected rabbi of Frankfurt-am-Main—a most important and prestigious rabbinical post—and remained there until his death in 1805. He was renowned for his learning and wrote two famous commentaries on selected passages from two tractates of the Talmud: one of these, the *Sefer Hafla'ah* or 'Book of Distinction', was so widely read and esteemed that Rabbi Pinchas was often known simply as 'the *Hafla'ah*'. He was the brother of Rabbi Schmelke of Nikolsburg, and both of them were disciples of Dov Baer, the Maggid of Mezritch, who was one of the leading lights and most important figures in early hasidism. It was Rabbi Schmelke who trained Moshe Leib of Sasov whom we have already met in these pages.

The German text of this story is to be found in Bloch, *Die Gemeinde der Chassidim* (see above, s.v. Moshe Leib of Sasov) 136–7.

Notes

Lakhovitch] Lakhovitch/Lechowitz/Lachowicze/Lyakhovichi was one of the most important centres of Lithuanian hasidism. It was (and still is) a small town quite close to Slutsk.

the World to Come] i.e. the eternal Kingdom of Heaven which, according to Talmudic teaching, follows the temporary reign of Messiah and which is ushered in by a general resurrection and judgment.

PISENTIUS OF QIFT

Pisentius was born about 568 and entered the monastery of Phoebammon, which probably lay a few miles northeast of Thebes. After some years he moved from there to another monastery close by, and from there to a small community near Der al-Bahri, the monastery (again at Thebes) which had been built on the Upper Terrace of the magnificent temple of Queen Hatshepsut (nothing remains of it today). In due course he was appointed bishop of Qift (the ancient Koptos) and consecrated in Alexandria by the patriarch Damian. The date must have been about 569. He governed his see, apparently with great success, for more than thirty years, but fled to the desert when Egypt was invaded by the Persians under Chosroes II in 616. After the Persians were expelled by Heraclius in 627, Pisentius returned from his seclusion and died sometime between this date and the Arab invasion some thirteen years later.

The Arabic text of the story translated here is to be found in De Lacy O'Leary, *The Arabic Life of Saint Pisentius* (*Patrologia Orientalis* XXII.3; Paris, 1930) 396.

POEMEN

Poemen, 'the shepherd', was a fairly common name among the dwellers in the desert, and nothing more is known of this one save the story narrated here. He is described as a *boskos*, a noun which derives from the Greek verb 'to graze', and I have therefore called him a 'grass-eater'. But he and those like him (for the term appears elsewhere) presumably supplemented their diet with other, more sustaining, animal fodder. At the time these events took place, Poemen was living in the Rouba desert, a most inhospitable tract of arid and rocky land between the Kastellion monastery and the Dead Sea. The narrator, Agathonicus, was *hegoumenos* of the Kastellion monastery, which was founded 492–493 in the ruins of the Kastellion/Castellium fortress (which appears to be the same as the Hyrcania fortress of Herodian fame), just a couple of miles from Mar Saba, the important lavra founded by Saint Sabas in 478.

The Greek text of the story is to be found in John Moschus, *Pratum Spirituale, cap.* 167; PL 87: 3033CD.

Notes

he was from the two Galatias] i.e. he came from what is now central Turkey.

RŪMĪ

Jalāl-ud-Dīn Rūmī, one of the very greatest of the world's spiritual teachers, was born in Balkh in 1207. His name—Jalāl-ud-Dīn—means 'the majesty, or splendour, or sublimity of religion', and the appellation Rūmī means 'of Rome', i.e. from that part of the eastern Roman empire which is now modern Turkey. His father, Bahā'-ud-Dīn, was a famous theologian and may have had a greater influence on Rūmī's own beliefs than has so far been recognised. Father and son moved to Konya in 1228 (the mother had died two years earlier) and settled in what was then one of the few places which offered some safety and security from the depredations of the Mongols. Many learned and literary figures had flocked there and the city was an intellectual, religious, cultural, and spiritual stronghold with a population both Muslim and Christian, and three main languages: Persian, Turkish, and Greek. Rūmī spent the rest of his life in Konya, though he travelled to Syria at least once in his quest for wisdom, and it is possible, though by no means certain, that he met there the mysterious and charismatic Shams-ud-Dīn of Tabrīz who was to have such a marked influence on him and his thought. Rūmī's own teaching centres on the mystery of divine love—God's love for us and ours for God—and finds its finest expression in his inspired masterwork, the great *Mathnawī-i ma'nawī*, of which a complete translation (by Reynold Nicholson) is available in English. He was also the founder of that order of sufis known to the west as the 'whirling dervishes', an order which, from an early period, exercised a fascination on european travellers to Turkey, and which contributed to Rūmī's fame in the west. He died on 17 December, 1273. A huge amount of information, both reliable and unreliable, on Rūmī and his order is provided by Shams-ud-Dīn Aḥmad al-Aflākī in his *Manāqib al-'ārifīn*, 'Eulogies of the Initiates', and it is from this mine of information that I have selected the anecdotes which appear in this present volume.

     For the Persian text, see Shams al-Dīn Aḥmad al-Aflākī al-'Ārifī, ed. Tahsin Yazici, *Manākib al-'ārifīn* (Türk Tarih Kurumu Yayinlarindan III. Seri, No. 3; Ankara, 1959–61), two volumes: for 'The Ass's Bray', see Vol. 1 pages 114–6 (sections 3/33–34); for the 'Canine Initiates', Vol. 1 pages 165–6 (section 3/76); for 'Greater love hath no cat...', Vol. 2 page 580 (section 3/566–567). I have sometimes abridged the translations, and sometimes added explanatory passages which may serve to clarify unfamiliar terms.

Notes

The Ass's Bray

our Master] *Maulana*: such is the title by which Rūmī's
followers have always referred to him.

in the community] 'in the *madrase/madrese* (Arabic
madrasa)': a *madrase* was (and is) a school, usually attached to
a mosque, in which some disciples would live and to which
others would come for instruction.

friends] the Persian word (Aflākī usually uses *yar*)
means more than just 'a friend' in the way we use it today: it is
a sort of technical term for the members of a sufi community.
The sufis, not only the Quakers, are the Society of Friends.

its genitals] Aflākī uses the Arabic loan-word *farj*, 'an
opening, breach, vulva', which would seem to indicate that
he is thinking of a female ass. This would certainly accord
with the view of women—a dangerous and libidinous breed,
best avoided—held by most pious Muslims of his day. Rūmī
makes it clear, however, that the moral of the story applies to
all of us.

a secret] this is what the text says, though what it
means is not at all clear. The Arabic loan-word *sirrī* certainly
means a secret, though we might also translate it as 'esoteric
knowledge'. In the phrase *asrār al-qur'ān*, it means 'the secret or
esoteric interpretation of the Qur'ān'.

concupiscence] *lit.* 'the inclinations of the *nafs*', and
the war against the *nafs*, or 'lower self', is at the heart of every
spiritual discipline. The *nafs* is the *propria voluntas* 'self-will'
of the Christian tradition, and is the source of all our sinful,
self-centred, and stupid actions. Judaism, Christianity, and
Islam are at one on this point: so long as we do what *we* want,
we are doomed; we must eradicate the 'us' and do what *God*
wants. As Athenagoras of Athens said in the second century:

we must become flutes on which God plays. This is the true Islam, the true 'submission', and the goal of all sufi teaching.

the country estate of Ḥusām-ud-Dīn Chelebī] for 'country estate', the Persian simply has 'garden'. Ḥusām-ud-Dīn was Rūmī's favourite disciple and, in due course, succeeded him as head of the Mevlevi order. He was probably born about 1226 and died at Konya in 1284. He was well-known for his devotion both to God and to Rūmī, and the high position he occupied in the eyes of the latter may have been partly due to the fact that he knew and respected Rūmī's teacher, Shams-ud-Dīn of Tabrīz, whose often unorthodox behaviour and acerbic tongue did not endear him to many. Ḥusām-ud-Dīn himself left no writings, but was responsible for persuading Rūmī to compose the *Mathnawī*; and in the preparation of this huge work he frequently acted as Rūmī's secretary, writing down the words as our Master uttered them, and then reading them back to him. Chelebī, finally, is a Turkish honorific which was applied to well-known men of letters from the early thirteenth century onwards, but from the time of Ḥusām-ud-Dīn, it was also the title born by the heads of the sufi orders. As a secular title in Turkey, it was replaced in the early 1700's by *effendi*.

blabbermouth] or 'blatherer, meddler, busybody' (the verse is in Arabic).

Canine Initiates

To appreciate this story one must remember that as far as Muslims are concerned, dogs are unclean animals. Contact with a dog requires ritual cleansing (any area which has been touched by a dog's saliva or other bodily effluent must be washed seven times, a little dust being mixed with the water), and in sufi literature we can find many examples of the despised *nafs*, the 'lower soul' which we spoke of above, being symbolised by a dog.

There is a famous tale of a outwardly pious man going into a mosque at sunset (making sure that everyone could see him) and spending the whole night in ostentatious prayer. He could hear some rustlings in the darkness, but presumed it was just another person, and he was quite happy to have a witness to his extravagant devotion. But when dawn broke, he found that his fellow-worshipper had been a dog, and his own prayers were therefore invalid and his own person ritually polluted. I should add that there is more than one point to this story, but it does illustrate the despised position held by dogs in Muslim lands.

Rūmī, however, teaches the dogs not just ordinary worldly knowledge, but *ma'rifa*, the esoteric, secret knowledge of the highest levels of the sufi path, and identifies them with the family of the dog of the Seven Sleepers. The reference here is to the legend of the Seven Sleepers of Ephesus: they were seven young Christian men who took refuge in a cave during the Decian persecution in the mid-  third century, and who were there walled up. Two centuries later (according to Christian tradition) they were awakened and came forth from their entombment hale and hearty, thus demonstrating the possibility of bodily resurrection. The story appears in the Qur'ān (18:9–13), but as a consequence of a mis-understanding and a misreading of an expression in Qur'ān 18:9, Muslim legend maintains that the Seven Sleepers were accompanied by their dog (his name was Raqīm according to earlier sources, and Qiṭmīr according to later ones). What Rūmī is doing, therefore, is elevating one of the most despised and rejected of animals not only to a position of equality with sufi initiates, but to a position worthy of commemoration and praise by God Himself.

whined very quietly] lit. 'saying quietly, quietly *zū,*
zū', which is what Persian dogs say when they are contented.
Anyone who has a dog will recognise the noise.

esoteric teaching] *ma'refat* 'gnosis'.

'Greater Love Hath No Cat . . .'

the Master's wife] her name was Jawhar Khatūn.

his blessed community] lit. 'his blessed *madrase'*.

SERGIUS THE ANCHORITE

Of the life of Sergius the Anchorite I can provide no
details, save what is told us in this brief account. The Greek
text of the anecdote is to be found in *caput* 125 of the *Pratum
Spirituale* of John Moschus, PL 87: 2987B-C.

Notes

a piece of blessed bread] in Greek, *eulogia.* The term
means simply 'blessing' and might refer to any number of
things. At an early period it could refer to the bread which
had actually been consecrated in the eucharist and was being
sent to absent members of the church as a symbol of its unity;
later, it could refer to the bread which had been blessed at the
eucharist, but not consecrated—the *panis benedictus*—and which
was distributed separately at the end of the Divine Liturgy.
Otherwise it could refer to bread which had been blessed at
any time—at a regular meal, for example—or even to bread
which had simply been in contact with some holy object. Finally, it might mean no more than a gift—alms, for instance,

or food given to senior members of the community. It is unclear, therefore, precisely what the lion ate, but it seems to have been effective.

SHENOUTE THE GREAT

Shenoute, who was born about 348 and died in advanced old age about 466, was one of the titan figures of Egyptian monasticism. That his name is generally unfamiliar in the west is a consequence of the fact that his sermons and treatises (of which there are a considerable number) were composed entirely in Coptic and were never (so far as we know) translated into Greek. Since they did not appear in Greek, they did not appear in Latin either; and the fame of this Egyptian abbot, who at one time governed thousands of monks and nuns from his spiritual centre at the White Monastery (a few miles from the modern town of Akhmim in Upper Egypt), remained confined to Egypt. Shenoute was certainly charismatic, but he could also be very violent (he beat one of his monks to death for a relatively minor infringement of his monastic rule); and although he was undoubtedly capable of arousing the most fervent devotion and love amongst his disciples, his personality is not to everyone's taste. On the other hand, he can exert a curious fascination: when I first began reading his works some years ago, I liked neither them nor him. But now I am one of his greatest admirers and staunchest defenders. Perhaps my visit to the church of Saint Shenoute had something to do with it. It is located just outside Old Cairo, and the right arm of the saint (with the fingers, I suspect, still clenched in a fist) is preserved just below a splendid icon of Shenoute and Besa. It was Besa (pronounced 'Visa'), Shenoute's disciple and successor as abbot, who wrote the life of the saint, and the story here translated—a story which illustrates a softer side of Shenoute— is taken (with some minor variants) from my own translation of the complete life: *Besa: The Life of Shenoute,* tr. D. N. Bell

(CS 73; Kalamazoo, 1983) 86 (sect. 161). For the Coptic text, see *Sinuthii Archimandritae Vita et Opera Omnia I*, ed. J. Leipoldt and W. E. Crum (CSCO Scriptores Coptici, Series Secunda, Tomus II; Paris, 1906) 68–9 (sect. 161).

SUFYĀN AL-THAURI

Abu 'Abd Allāh Sufyān ibn Sa'id al-Thauri was born at Kufa in 715 and became famous for his knowledge of *ḥadīth* (the multitudinous traditions which record the words and deeds of Muḥammad) and theology. But there is no doubt that had he known of him, Sufyān would have agreed with Evagrius Ponticus, that a theologian is someone who truly prays, and someone who truly prays is a theologian. His own life bore eloquent testimony to his whole-hearted devotion to God as well as his compassion for God's creatures, and after his death in 778 he was revered by the Sufis as a saint. On one occasion Sufyān was eating some bread when a dog happened to come by (and it must be remembered that dogs are unclean animals for Muslims). Thereupon Sufyān broke the bread in

pieces and gave it to the dog. When those nearby saw this, they asked him: 'Why don't you share it with your wife and child?' 'If I give it to the dog,' said Sufyān, 'he'll guard me all night so that I can pray; but if I give it to my wife and child, they'll distract my mind from my dèvotions.' It all depends, obviously, on who comes first.

The Persian text of the story of the little bird is to be found in Farīduddīn 'Aṭṭār's *Tadhkiratu'l-Awliya* (see above s.v. Nūrī) I: 195 line 20–196 line 3.

SYMEON THE ELDER

Symeon the Elder is so called to distinguish him from the more famous pillar-saint, Symeon the Younger, better known as Simon Stylites. The elder Symeon first lived as a hermit in the wilderness east of Cyrrhus (some distance northeast of Antioch in Syria) but sometime later, perhaps about 370, he moved closer to the city and took up residence just to the north of it, on the southern slopes of Mount Amanus. There he converted the local inhabitants to Christianity and established two monasteries, one near the top of the mountain and one at the bottom. After a life of what, for Syria, was fairly standard asceticism (and what for us would be savage and extraordinary torment and deprivation), he died about 390.

The Greek text of both stories is to be found in *Théodoret de Cyr, Histoire des moines de Syrie: Histoire Philothée I-XIII*, ed./tr. P. Canivet and A. Leroy-Molinghen (SCh 234; Paris, 1977) I: 348–50 (VI:2; guiding the travellers) and 358–60 (VI:9–10; the ascetic and the lion). The whole *History* is now available in an excellent English translation by R. M. Price: *Theodoret of Cyrrhus: A History of the Monks of Syria* (CS 88; Kalamazoo, 1985).

Notes

Guiding the Travellers

one of the fortresses] one of the Roman border fortresses guarding the boundaries of the province of Syria.

covered in dirt and filth] a refusal to wash or in any way clean oneself was a standard feature of Syrian asceticism.

TATHAN

Tathan, Tatheus, Tathai, or Tathar was a young man of Irish ancestry who, on receiving a command from an angel, sailed to South Wales with a small group of disciples. Here, at the instigation of the local ruler, Caradog, he founded a monastic school at Caerwent which achieved considerable fame. He was also responsible for other foundations, but precisely which and exactly how many remains unclear. According to his *Life*, he died at Caerwent and was buried under the floor of the church which he had founded, and in a series of excavations conducted in 1911 a skeleton was found which may, indeed, have been that of the saint. On this assumption, the bones were removed to the parish church and there reburied. Tathan's cult was never large (his feast-day is 26 December) and his dates remain obscure: he might have flourished at almost any time during the fifth or sixth centuries.

The Latin texts of both stories are to be found in Wade-Evans, *Vitae Sanctorum Britanniae et Genealogiae* (see above s.v. Brynach), 282 (Tathan and his pet doves) and 283–4 (the story of the wolf and the pigs). The poem at the end of the first tale is in Leonine hexameters.

THEON

Apart from the story and the summary which I have presented here, nothing further is known of Theon.

The Greek text of the account is to be found in the *Historia Monachorum in Aegypto* VI,4 (page 45 in Festugière's edition: see above s.v. Helle).

WERBURGA OF CHESTER

Werburga is said to have been the daughter of Wulf-
here, king of Mercia, and after the death of her father, she
became a nun at Ely under the abbess and former queen Ethel-
dreda (who was also, in due course, to be canonized). Ethel-
dreda was succeeded as abbess by Sexburga (also a saint),
Sexburga by Ermengild (yet another saint and also Werburga's
mother), and Ermengild—possibly but not certainly—by Werburga herself. Werburga was responsible for founding or re-
forming a number of nunneries in the English midlands and
it was at one of these that she died, after a life of singularly
active sanctity, about the year 700. She was originally buried at
Hanbury (another of her foundations), but her relics were later
translated to Chester to keep them out of the way of maraud-
ing Danes. Chester Cathedral is dedicated to her, and her feast
day is 3 February. The story of the resurrected goose actually
belongs to another saint—Amelburga—but it has been associated with Werburga for almost a thousand years and normally
appears as her emblem.

The Latin text of this version of the story is to be found
in William of Malmesbury, ed. N. E. S. A. Hamilton, *De Gestis
Pontificum Anglorum* (Rolls Series 52; London, 1870) 308–9
(Book IV, section 172).

WULFSTAN OF WORCESTER

Wulfstan or Wulstan was a remarkable man. He was
born into an Anglo-Saxon family and educated at the abbeys
of Evesham and Peterborough. After his ordination, he was
offered a rich and important living, but preferred to enter the
Benedictine priory at Worcester. By about 1050 he had become
prior, and some twelve years later, in 1062, he was consecrated

bishop of Worcester. He was an excellent administrator: far-
sighted, active, judicious, zealous, energetic; and at the same
time, a truly devout monk: learned, generous, honest, and ab-
stemious. He naturally became involved in the political turmoil
of his times, and after the Norman Conquest in 1066 he offered
his allegiance to William the Conqueror. As a reward (and
also as a consequence of his outstanding abilities) he was one
of the few Anglo-Saxon prelates to retain his episcopal office
under William and his successors. He died in 1095 when he
was nearly ninety and is buried in Worcester Cathedral. His
feast day is 19 January.

The Latin text of this anecdote is to be found in William of Malmesbury, *De Gestis Pontificum Anglorum* (see above
s.v. Werburga of Chester) 282–3 (Book IV, section 141). William
also wrote a full-length and detailed life of the saint which has
been translated into English by J. H. F. Peile, *William of Malmesbury's Life of St. Wulstan, Bishop of Worcester* (Oxford, 1934).

ZEV WOLF OF ZBARAZH

Rabbi Wolf of Zbarazh (a small town formerly in East
Galicia, but now part of Ukrainia) was the son of Rabbi Yechiel
Mikhal, the Maggid of Zlotzov/Zlotchov, who was one of the
three greatest disciples of the Baal Shem Tov, the founder of
hasidism. Rabbi Mikhal was a severe and austere figure, as
harsh with himself as with others, and noted for the sever-
ity of his penances. It was said of him that he never warmed
himself at the stove (to do so would have been a concession
to indolence), never bent his head to his food, (to do so would
have been a concession to greed), and never scratched himself
(to do so would have been a concession to comfort). His son
Zev, however, was quite different. Perhaps as a reaction to the
asceticism of his father he was known for his love of people
and animals, and refused to make any distinction in his love

between the good and the wicked. That, after all, was up to God. Once, when one of his disciples complained to him that certain people in the town were staying up all night playing cards and carousing, Rabbi Wolf said that it was a good thing. 'They're like everybody else,' he said. 'They want to serve God, but they don't know how. But now they're learning how to stay awake and devote themselves to something, and when they can do this really well, all they need to do is to direct it to God instead of cards. And then—just think!—what excellent servants they will be!' On another occasion, Rabbi Wolf was travelling to a nearby town and his driver started to lash the horses so that they would go more quickly. 'Don't hit them,' said the rabbi, 'indeed, if you knew how to talk to them properly, you wouldn't even need to shout at them.'

The German text of this present story is to be found in Bloch, *Die Gemeinde der Chassidim* (see above, s.v. Moshe Leib of Sasov) 259.

INDEX OF ANIMALS

CISTERCIAN PUBLICATIONS, INC.
TITLES LISTINGS

CISTERCIAN TEXTS

THE WORKS OF BERNARD OF CLAIRVAUX

Apologia to Abbot William
Five Books on Consideration: Advice to a Pope
Grace and Free Choice
Homilies in Praise of the Blessed Virgin Mary
The Life and Death of Saint Malachy the Irishman
Love without Measure. Extracts from the Writings
    of St Bernard (Paul Dimier)
The Parables of Saint Bernard (Michael Casey)
Sermons for the Summer Season
Sermons on the Song of Songs I - IV
Steps of Humility and Pride

THE WORKS OF WILLIAM OF SAINT THIERRY

The Enigma of Faith
Exposition on the Epistle to the Romans
The Golden Epistle
The Mirror of Faith
The Nature and Dignity of Love

THE WORKS OF AELRED OF RIEVAULX

Dialogue on the Soul
The Mirror of Charity
Spiritual Friendship
Treatises I: On Jesus at the Age of Twelve, Rule for
    a Recluse, The Pastoral Prayer

THE WORKS OF JOHN OF FORD

Sermons on the Final Verses of the Song of
    Songs I - VII

THE WORKS OF GILBERT OF HOYLAND

Sermons on the Songs of Songs I-III
Treatises, Sermons and Epistles

OTHER EARLY CISTERCIAN WRITERS

The Letters of Adam of Perseigne I
Baldwin of Ford: Spiritual Tractates I - II
Gertrud the Great of Helfta: Spiritual Exercises
Gertrud the Great of Helfta: The Herald of God's
    Loving-Kindness
Guerric of Igny: Liturgical Sermons I - II
Idung of Prüfening: Cistercians and Cluniacs: The
    Case of Cîteaux
Isaac of Stella: Sermons on the Christian Year
Serlo of Wilton & Serlo of Savigny
Stephen of Lexington: Letters from Ireland
Stephen of Sawley: Treatises

MONASTIC TEXTS

EASTERN CHRISTIAN TRADITION

Besa: The Life of Shenoute
Cyril of Scythopolis: Lives of the Monks of Palestine
Dorotheos of Gaza: Discourses
Evagrius Ponticus:Praktikos and Chapters on
    Prayer

The Harlots of the Desert (Benedicta Ward)
Iosif Volotsky: Monastic Rule
The Lives of the Desert Fathers
Mena of Nikiou: Isaac of Alexandra &
    St Macrobius
Pachomian Koinonia I - III
The Sayings of the Desert Fathers
    Spiritual Direction in the Early Christian East
    (Irénée Hausherr)
The Syriac Fathers on Prayer and the Spiritual Life
    (Sebastian Brock)

WESTERN CHRISTIAN TRADITION

Anselm of Canterbury: Letters I - [III]
Bede: Commentary on the Seven Catholic Epistles
Bede: Commentary on the Acts of the Apostles
Bede: Gospel Homilies I - II
Bede: Homilies on the Gospels I - II
Cassian: Conferences I - III
Gregory the Great: Forty Gospel Homilies
Guigo II the Carthusian: Ladder of Monks and
    Twelve Mediations
Peter of Celle: Selected Works
The Letters of Armand-Jean de Rance I - II
The Life of Beatrice of Nazareth
The Rule of the Master

CHRISTIAN SPIRITUALITY

Abba: Guides to Wholeness & Holiness East & West
A Cloud of Witnesses: The Development of
    Christian Doctrine (D.N. Bell)
Athirst for God: Spiritual Desire in Bernard of
    Clairvaux's Sermons on the Song of Songs
    (M. Casey)
Cistercian Way (André Louf)
Fathers Talking (Aelred Squire)
Friendship and Community (B. McGuire)
From Cloister to Classroom
Herald of Unity: The Life of Maria Gabrielle
    Sagheddu (M. Driscoll)
Life of St Mary Magdalene and of Her Sister St
    Martha (D. Mycoff)
The Name of Jesus (Irénée Hausherr)
Penthos: The Doctrine of Compunction in the
    Christian East (Irénée Hausherr)
Rancé and the Trappist Legacy (A.J. Krailsheimer)
The Roots of the Modern Christian Tradition
Russian Mystics (S. Bolshakoff)
The Spirituality of the Christian East (Tomas
    Spidlék)

MONASTIC STUDIES

Community & Abbot in the Rule of St Benedict
    I - II (Adalbert De Vogüé)
Beatrice of Nazareth in Her Context (Roger
    De Ganck)
Consider Your Call: A Theology of the Monastic
    Life (Daniel Rees et al.)
The Finances of the Cistercian Order in the Four
    teenth Century (Peter King)
Fountains Abbey & Its Benefactors (Joan Wardrop)
The Hermit Monks of Grandmont (Carole A.
    Hutchison)

TITLES LISTINGS

Cistercian Publications is a non-profit corporation.
Its publishing program is restricted to monastic
texts in translation and books on the monastic
tradtion.

*North American customers may order these books
through booksellers or directly from the warehouse:*
Cistercian Publications
St Joseph's Abbey
Spencer, Massachusetts 01562
(508) 885-7011
fax 508-885-4687

British and European customers may order these
books through booksellers or from:
Brian Griffin
Storey House, White Cross
South Road, Lancaster LA1 4QX
England

*Editorial queries and advance book information should be
directed to the Editorial Offices:*
Cistercian Publications
Institute of Cistercian Studies
Western Michigan University
Kalamazoo, Michigan 49008
(616) 387-8920

*A complete catalogue of texts in translation and studies
on early, medieval, and modern monasticism is available
at no cost from Cistercian Publications.*